SO-BSR-459

USING TECHNOLOGY
TO
SUPPORT EDUCATION REFORM

Barbara Means
John Blando
Kerry Olson
Teresa Middleton
SRI International

Catherine Cobb Morocco
Arlene R. Remz
Judith Zorfass
Education Development Corporation

U.S. Department of Education
Richard W. Riley
Secretary

Office of Educational Research and Improvement
Sharon P. Robinson
Assistant Secretary

Office of Research
Joseph C. Conaty
Acting Director

Q
371.3
U 85

September 1993

The conduct of this study and preparation of this report
were sponsored by the U.S. Department of Education,
Office of Educational Research and Improvement, under
Contract No. RR91172010. Any opinions, findings,
conclusions, or recommendations expressed in this
publication are those of the authors and do not
necessarily reflect the views of the U.S. Department of
Education.

For sale by the U.S. Government Printing Office
Superintendent of Documents, Mail Stop: SSOP, Washington, DC 20402-9328
ISBN 0-16-042048-2

Contents

Tables

Figures

Chapter 1
Introduction

Political leaders, employers, and the public are expressing an unprecedented level of concern with the state of education in America. Since the stark warning in *A Nation at Risk* that the erosion of educational standards "threatens our very future as a Nation and a people," we have seen a proliferation of education reform efforts. Most prevalent during the 1980s were efforts aimed at raising course requirements and scores on standardized achievement tests. Critics have characterized these earlier reform efforts as quantitative rather than qualitative in nature (i.e., "more of the same"). The result was an increase in the number of school courses with advanced academic titles, but the nature of instruction remained unchanged and course content often failed to live up to course titles. Achievement of more advanced skills in subject areas showed no discernible gains.

Currently, prevailing opinion is that piecemeal attempts at reform get swallowed up by the multiple levels and component parts of an education system that perpetuates the status quo and that if we want drastic improvements, we will have to undertake fundamental and comprehensive change (Smith & O'Day, 1990). A new willingness to consider fundamental change and innovative approaches is apparent in the current wave of reform efforts that are involving governors and state legislatures, business coalitions, and others as well as educators themselves including teachers' associations, colleges of education, and school administrators. Educators, policy makers, and citizens are now seriously debating kinds of structural reforms that would have seemed wildly idealistic just a decade ago.

Many critics of American schools see technology as an important tool in bringing about the kind of revolutionary changes called for in these new reform efforts. Having seen the ways in which technology has transformed the workplace, and, indeed, most of our communications and commercial activities, the business community and the public in general are exerting pressure for comparable changes within schools.

Thus, support for the use of technology to promote fundamental school reform appears to be reaching a new high. At the same time, we have the opportunity to profit from the experiences of those educational institutions that already have implemented various technological innovations within the context of serious reform efforts. In these cases, technology is viewed as a means of supporting goals related to increased student involvement with complex, authentic tasks and new organizational structures within classrooms and schools (Sheingold, 1990).

The primary motivation for using technologies in education is the belief that they will support superior forms of learning. For this reason, theory and research in learning provide an extremely important source of ideas. Advances in cognitive psychology have sharpened our understanding of the nature of skilled intellectual performance and provide a basis for designing environments conducive to learning. There is now a widespread agreement among educators and psychologists (Collins, Brown & Newman 1989; Resnick 1987) that advanced skills of comprehension, reasoning, composition, and experimentation are acquired not through the transmission of facts but through the learner's interaction with content. This *constructivist* view of learning, with its call for teaching basic skills within authentic contexts (hence more complex problems), for modeling expert thought processes, and for providing for collaboration and external supports to permit students to achieve intellectual accomplishments they could not do on their own, provides the wellspring of ideas for many of this decade's curriculum and instruction reform efforts.

Concurrently, we are at a time of great technological advance. Computing power is more available and affordable than ever before. Satellite transmission can beam instructional material to sites thousands of miles away. Computer graphics can create "virtual environments" in which the individual sees and interacts with an artificial three-dimensional world. Tools to support computer applications make it possible for school children to do everything from communicating with their counterparts on the other side of the world to building their own curriculum materials in hypermedia formats to collecting and analyzing data much as practicing scientists would. While the most sophisticated technology remains in the hands of the few, it is becoming more and more affordable and available. At the same time, we are finding educationally sophisticated uses of commonplace technologies, such as videotape and word processing.

Over the years, educators have heard enough drum beating to become jaded about technologies' ability to transform the school. Yet, there are enough cases where technology and school reform have been successful partners to tell us that the marriage can be a productive one (Sheingold & Tucker 1990; Stearns et al. 1991; Zorfass 1991). On the other side of the coin, there are many cases where school districts invested in technology that turned out not to be well used (computers gathering dust in the corner of a classroom), or to be used in ways that merely perpetuated the status quo (e.g., Mehan 1989; Oakes & Schneider 1984). From the "successes" we have learned that technology often produces unexpected benefits for students and teachers (Stearns et al. 1991). From "failures" we have learned that implementation without thoughtful planning or sustained support is nearly always futile.

Elements of School Reform

The experience of the last decade tells us that serious reform efforts must look not just at the classroom but at the whole system within which education takes place. Nevertheless, the ultimate goal is to have a beneficial impact on students, and that is where we will begin in describing our framework for thinking about school reform.

Student-Level Elements

Although variously described, the student-level outcome goals of most reform efforts are to increase learning, especially of advanced or higher-level skills, and to enhance student motivation and self-concept. Naturally, there are various schools of thought as to how to achieve these ends, but the dominant thinking within the reform movement appears to stress the elements shown in the second column of Table I-1.

Table I-1

COMPARISON OF CONVENTIONAL AND REFORM APPROACHES TO INSTRUCTION

Conventional Instruction	Reform Instruction
Teacher-directed	Student exploration
Didactic teaching	Interactive modes of instruction
Short blocks of instruction on single subject	Extended blocks of authentic and multidisciplinary work
Individual work	Collaborative work
Teacher as knowledge dispenser	Teacher as facilitator
Ability groupings	Heterogeneous groupings
Assessment of fact knowledge and discrete skills	Performance-based assessment

In our view, the catalyst for this transformation is centering instruction around *authentic, challenging tasks* (see Figure I-1). There is a strong sense that schools have broken down tasks into discrete component skills that have no obvious connection with anything students do outside of school (e.g., learning algorithms for finding square roots). This practice has negative effects on motivation and makes transfer of learned skills to real-world tasks unlikely (Resnick 1987).

Reformers argue that students should be given tasks that are personally meaningful and challenging to them (e.g., describe their city to students in another part of the world). Meaningful tasks almost always will be more complex than the tasks assigned with a discrete-skills approach, and they also will tend to be *multidisciplinary* (e.g., describing the city means assembling geographic and historic facts as well as working on composition skills), a

Figure I-1.—Authentic, Challenging Tasks as the Core of Education Reform

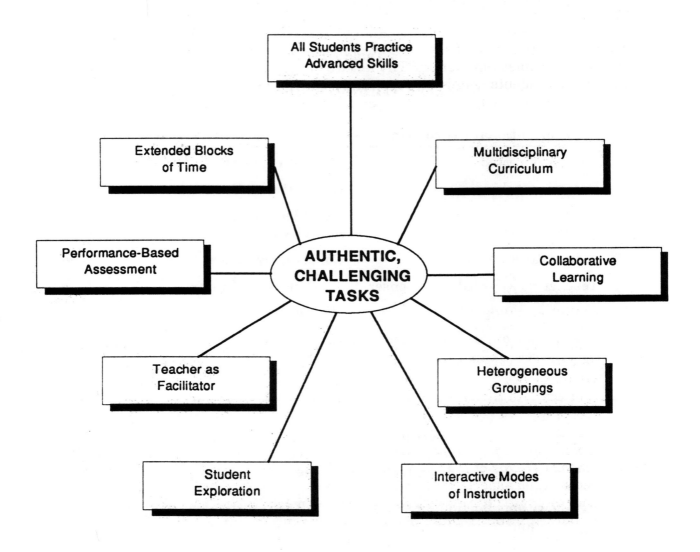

feature that conflicts with the standard middle and secondary school structure of distinct disciplines. Further, the fact that the tasks will be more complex suggests that longer blocks of time will be required to work on them, again conflicting with the notion of 50-minute periods for distinct subject areas.

Given these complex tasks, students take a more active part in defining their own learning goals and regulating their own learning. *Students explore* ideas and bodies of knowledge, not in order to repeat back verbal formalisms on demand, but to understand phenomena and find information they need for their project work. When working on complex tasks, student work will often cross over the borders of academic disciplines, just as real-world problems often demand the application of several kinds of expertise. In this context, instruction becomes *interactive*. The nature of the information and the support provided for students change depending on what students do; the problems they work on can change and evolve over time.

These complex tasks also lend themselves to *collaborative work*. Some students track down all the economic data on their city, while others look into information on weather patterns. Students work through mathematics problems as a group or serve as each other's editor when writing documents. There are many advantages of collaborative learning (see, for example, Lesgold et al. 1992).

In the process of collaborating, students gain experience in negotiating the purpose of their work, the meaning of the terms they use, and so on. These experiences mirror the activities of professionals working together. Collaborative work also has advantages in terms of motivation: students get involved because they like to work together; further, if difficulties encountered are temporarily daunting to one student, another student's enthusiasm can carry the work forward. Another frequently noted advantage for peer collaboration is the fact that it calls on students to justify their conclusions and to act as external critics for each other. In so doing, they become more reflective about their own thinking. Over time, students come to internalize the role of critic so that they can act as critic for their own work.

Collaborative projects facilitate adjusting tasks to accommodate individual differences. Students of different ability levels can work together, taking roles commensurate with their skills. Thus, it becomes feasible to teach *heterogeneous groups* of students who vary in age, expertise (e.g., each group may need a video expert), ability levels, and so on. Within such groups, the experience of explaining something to a fellow student who does not understand it can in itself be educationally valuable.

Within this learning model, the *teacher becomes a facilitator and "coach"* rather than knowledge dispenser or project director. Teachers are responsible for setting up the inquiry units and creating the organizational structure within which groups do their work, but once work begins, teachers no longer have the total control of the direction of instruction that they exercise in conventional classrooms.

School Reform, Advanced Skills, and Disadvantaged Students

While the vision of a transformed classroom offered by reformers is important for all students, the change in practice would be especially dramatic for those who have been variously characterized as "disadvantaged" or "at–risk." An increasing number of the children in America's schools come from homes with incomes below the poverty line. Many have been raised in homes where English is not the dominant language or is not spoken at all. Others come from homes with only a single parent or from situations where there is little stability in terms of caregivers. Others must cope with physical, mental, or emotional disabilities. Statistically, students with these characteristics are more likely to fall behind in academic achievement, to drop out of school, or to turn off from the whole process of education.

The conventional view for these students has been one of diminished expectations—we have hoped to teach them the basic skills but have not expected them to attain high levels of accomplishment in the advanced skills of problem solving, scientific inquiry, or composition. As a consequence, curricula for these students have stressed discrete skills, with extensive drill and practice on vocabulary, number facts, and writing mechanics. In effect, we have given them less instruction on advanced skills, and less opportunity to develop capabilities in these areas, which are, in fact, those most important for their future lives.

In the new vision of reformed schools, these students would experience a dramatically different kind of classroom. Instead of treating basic skills as a hurdle that must be surmounted before attempting more complex tasks that involve reasoning, problem solving, and composition, disadvantaged students would learn basic skills in the context of working on challenging, authentic tasks (Means, Chelemer & Knapp 1991). Rather than emphasizing the practice of discrete skills such as spelling and punctuation on endless worksheets, the curriculum of disadvantaged students would stress composition, comprehension, and applications of skills. Rather than working in isolation, often in ability groupings or pull-out classes for compensatory instruction, disadvantaged students would work in mixed-ability groupings, often of mixed ages. They would be judged on their ability to perform a complex task and to reflect on and describe the thinking that went into it rather than on their facility with multiple-choice tests. One of the basic messages of school reform is that challenging problems and sustained intellectual effort are appropriate for all students, not just the academically advanced, affluent, or older ones.

Broader Context

An important lesson from earlier efforts to enhance students' learning is that one cannot simply intervene at the student level by providing a new curriculum or an advanced technology. Student learning occurs in a classroom with its own organizational structure, rules, and agenda. The classroom in turn is a unit within a school that provides the broader setting within which teachers and students must function. Policies, resources, restrictions, and mandates from the district, state, and federal levels likewise affect what happens in schools. Figure I-2 displays the components of education reform within this broader context.

School Level—The extensive literature on school reform efforts (see David & Shields 1991 for a review) can be characterized in terms of a small set of recurring themes.

Clear goals. Successful efforts at improving schools are characterized by a clear set of goals that are communicated to teachers, students, and parents alike. The earnest desire to improve is not enough; there needs to be a consensus concerning just what is to be improved and how that improvement will be measured.

Culture for learning. Schools, like corporations, have an organizational culture that embodies a set of values and sets up expectations for behavior. Changing schools means changing their culture. Elements of the culture associated with effective schools include high expectations (Brophy 1987), an atmosphere of collegiality (Rosenholtz 1985), and respect for—and links to—students' home lives and cultural communities (Comer 1988; Shields 1990).

Site-based management. An important element of new reform efforts is the decentralization of decision-making to the schools. Although held accountable for achieving outcomes, schools assume responsibility for making decisions about how to meet those goals. This requires effective leadership at the school level, and numerous studies document the importance of the principal in motivating faculty, influencing instruction, and managing the allocation of time (David & Shields 1991). Teachers, too, assume greater management responsibility as they work together to develop new curricula and evaluation practices and to provide new knowledge and coaching for each other (Fullan 1990).

Professionalization of teachers. A related component of reform is the magnification of the responsibilities and authority of teachers (Holmes Group 1990; Shulman 1986). In addition to the increased leadership role discussed above, reform efforts provide teachers with the opportunity to decide what and how to teach within their classrooms. The student learning model described above brings with it a new role for the teacher. Rather than following a textbook curriculum and telling students what they should know, the teacher develops meaningful tasks for students to work on and acts as a knowledge resource and "coach" who demonstrates intellectual skills, supports students as they try them out, and diagnoses weaknesses (Collins, Hawkins & Carver 1991). This role calls for a much higher degree of skill on the teacher's part and needs to be supported by opportunities to receive training and feedback in implementing new approaches (Knapp, Means & Chelemer 1991).

District, State, and Federal Levels—Although there are differences in the usual activities at the various levels of the educational system, the major functions in supporting reform are similar and can be discussed together for the sake of brevity. The site-based management discussed above clearly

Figure I-2.—Components of Education Reform

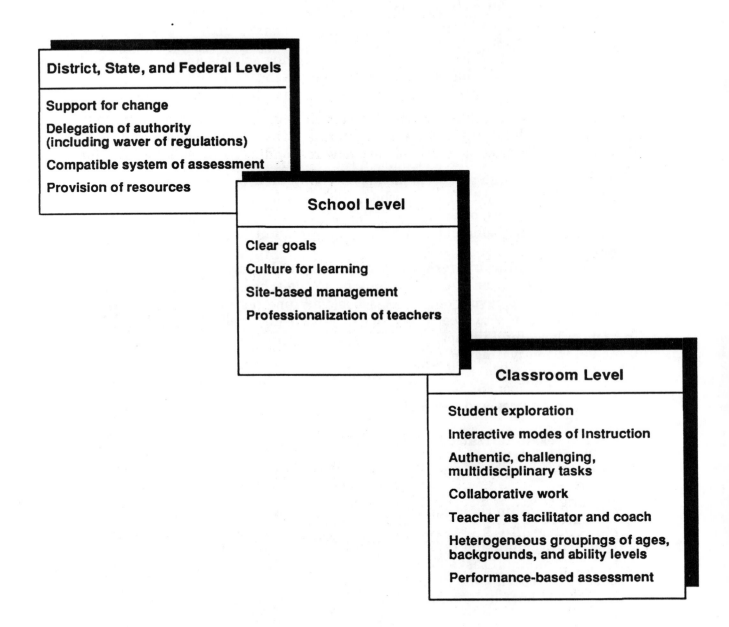

District, State, and Federal Levels

Support for change

Delegation of authority
(including waver of regulations)

Compatible system of assessment

Provision of resources

School Level

Clear goals

Culture for learning

Site-based management

Professionalization of teachers

Classroom Level

Student exploration

Interactive modes of Instruction

Authentic, challenging,
multidisciplinary tasks

Collaborative work

Teacher as facilitator and coach

Heterogeneous groupings of ages,
backgrounds, and ability levels

Performance-based assessment

requires that higher levels of bureaucracy *delegate authority*. This does not free the local entities from accountability, but merely gives them flexibility in making decisions and choosing means to meet specified ends. In many cases, this entails waiving state or federal regulations to allow innovative programs.

At the same time, district, state, and federal offices can support reform by *exercising leadership*. Schools are unlikely to change unless given a vision of what they could become and an incentive for restructuring (David 1989). Higher levels of the education system can provide support for change by articulating goals compatible with reform. The National Education Goals agreed to by the President and nation's Governors in 1990 highlighted the need for dramatic action. States are passing reform legislation, and some are calling for more local initiative (e.g., California, Minnesota, Virginia and Washington). Districts and schools are now responding to these mandates for innovation.

Innovation and reform are compatible with holding local schools and districts responsible for outcomes, but the accountability system needs to allow for *assessment compatible with the goals* of reform. In the past, accountability systems have tended to look predominantly at student scores on standardized tests stressing basic skills. Holding districts and schools accountable for these scores tended to stifle innovation, making schools reluctant to risk instituting programs emphasizing higher-order thinking skills. Instead of multiple-choice tests, innovative programs are seeking to measure student achievement in terms of exhibits, portfolios, and performances. Assessment systems that allow schools to use measures that are consistent with the goals of their innovations increase the likelihood that schools will try new approaches and improve our ability to document and measure the results of efforts to improve higher-order skills.

Educational improvement requires *resources*, most notably time for teachers to plan and develop programs and to receive and provide training in their implementation. This translates into dollars, and one of the major ways in which higher levels of the system contribute to reform is through provision of resources. These levels also provide technical assistance and opportunities for training teachers and administrators.

External Players—The above discussion of the elements of reform within the various levels of the education system should not be construed as the total picture. Many groups outside the education system per se are having an increasing role, not only in calling for reforms but in affecting their shape. The education system responds to pressures from political constituencies and is affected by state health and welfare policies. Businesses, both individual companies and interest groups, are becoming significant players in education reform, particularly in the case of reforms involving technologies, for which businesses constitute both potential donors and sources of technical expertise. Teacher education institutions are another key player outside the system. Teachers tend to teach the way that they were taught, and these institutions can do much to facilitate or impede the pace of reform. Finally, many reform efforts call for an increased involvement of parents in designing and fostering their children's schooling.

How Technology and Reform Fit Together: Contents of This Review

Technology and reform do not necessarily go hand in hand. Broad demonstrations of this fact are offered by all of the technologies that were going to revolutionize the classroom—television in the 1960s, computers in the 1970s, videodisc and artificial intelligence in the 1980s—but did not. More selective demonstrations of this fact are provided by studies of specific sites that invested in technology with the idea of changing the school or the classroom, only to find that the equipment sat in a closet or that teachers used the technology to do the same things they had always done (Oakes & Schneider 1984). At the same time, the majority of school reform efforts are proceeding without any appreciable contribution from technology (Ray 1991).

Nevertheless, studies of instructional uses of technology over the past decade have taken a new turn, showing not just whether a technology can teach or how it compares with conventional instruction (the focus of the earlier research literature) but the effects that technology has on what is learned and the teaching and learning roles within the classroom. What this literature shows, in brief, is that when used in ways that are compatible with the student learning model shown as the second column of Table I-1, technology supports exactly the kinds of changes in content, roles, organizational climate, and affect that are at the heart of the reform movement.

After reviewing the range of educational technologies used in education in Chapter II, we will turn to a description of how technology can support the kinds of student learning activities depicted in our model in Table I-1. In an area as multifaceted and fast changing as instructional technologies, an exhaustive review is not possible. Rather, we have attempted to convey a sense of the range of applications along with a more detailed description of selected programs that illustrate key points. Chapter III describes ways in which technology can support the kind of student learning activities called for by education reformers. Chapter IV describes ways in which technology can support the teacher activities needed to promote this kind of student learning. A discussion of the research literature on the effects of technology on student learning outcomes is presented in Chapter V. The final chapter deals with issues of implementation for projects attempting education reform supported by technology.

Chapter II
Educational Technologies

Educational technologies are not single technologies but complex combinations of hardware and software. These technologies may employ some combination of audio channels, computer code, data, graphics, video, or text. Although technology applications are frequently characterized in terms of their most obvious hardware feature (e.g., a VCR or a computer), from the standpoint of education, it is the nature of the instruction delivered that is important rather than the equipment delivering it. In this chapter, we review the history and current status of educational technologies, categorized into four basic uses: tutorial, exploratory, application, and communication. Our categories are designed to highlight differences in the instructional purposes of various technology applications, but we recognize that purposes are not always distinct, and a particular application may in fact be used in several of these ways.

Tutorial uses are those in which the technology does the teaching, typically in a lecture-like or workbook-like format in which the system controls what material will be presented to the student. In our classification scheme, tutorial uses include (1) expository learning, in which the system provides information; (2) demonstration, in which the system displays a phenomenon; and (3) practice, in which the system requires the student to solve problems, answer questions, or engage in some other procedure.

Exploratory uses of technology are those in which the student is free to roam around the information displayed or presented in the medium. Exploratory applications may promote discovery or guided discovery approaches to helping students learn information, knowledge, facts, concepts, or procedures. We also include reference applications, such as CD-ROM encyclopedias, in this category. In contrast to tutorial uses in which the technology acts on the student, in exploratory uses the student controls the learning (as in exploring microworlds or hypermedia stacks).

Application uses, such as word processors and spreadsheets, help students in the educational process by providing them with *tools* to facilitate writing tasks, analysis of data, and other uses. In addition to word processors and spreadsheets, applications include database management programs, graphing software, desktop publishing systems, and videotape recording and editing equipment.

Communication uses are those that allow students and teachers to send and receive messages and information to one another through networks or other technologies. Interactive distance learning via satellite, computer and modem, cable links, or other technologies constitutes another example of communication uses.

Table II-1 summarizes our technology classification scheme. Each of these four uses of technology in education is discussed below. A brief history of the technology use is presented, along with specific examples. A variety of media (e.g., computers, videodisc, audio) may be involved in any of these educational uses, sometimes stand-alone, other times in hybrid technology

Table II-1.—Classification of Education Technologies

Category	Definition	Examples
Tutorial	Systems designed to teach by providing information, demonstrations, or simulations in a sequence determined by the system. Tutorial systems may provide for expository learning (the system displays a phenomenon or procedure) and practice (the system requires the student to answer questions or solve problems).	Computer-assisted instruction (CAI) Intelligent CAI Instructional television Some videodisc/multimedia systems
Exploratory	Systems designed to facilitate student learning by providing information, demonstrations, or simulations when requested to do so by the student. Under student control, the system provides the context for discovery (or guided discovery) of facts, concepts, or procedures.	Microcomputer-based laboratories Microworlds/simulations Some videodisc/multimedia systems
Application	General-purpose tools for accomplishing tasks such as composition, data storage, or data analysis	Word processing software Spreadsheet software Database software Desktop publishing systems Video recording and editing equipment
Communication	Systems that allow groups of teachers and students to send information and data to each other through networks or other technologies.	Local area networks Wide area networks Interactive distance learning

systems. Under each use, we stress examples of technology applications that are well suited for teaching advanced thinking skills, especially with educationally disadvantaged students. Finally, this survey of technologies for education concludes with a review of the availability of these technologies in schools.

Technologies for Tutorial Learning

Historically, the dominant teaching-learning model has been one of transmission: teachers transmitting information to students. Not surprisingly, the first uses of educational technology supported this mode. Although other ways of using technology to support learning are now available, tutorial uses continue to be the most widespread, especially with disadvantaged students (Becker 1990).

Computer-Based Technologies

Computer-Assisted Instruction—Some of the first computer-assisted instruction (CAI), developed by Patrick Suppes at Stanford University during the 1960s, set standards for subsequent instructional software. After systematically analyzing courses in arithmetic and other subjects, Suppes designed highly structured computer systems featuring learner feedback, lesson branching, and student record keeping (Coburn et al. 1982).

During the 1970s, a particularly widespread and influential source of computer-assisted instruction was the University of Illinois' PLATO system. This system included hundreds of tutorial and drill-and-practice programs. Like other systems of the time, PLATO's resources were available through timesharing on a mainframe computer (Coburn et al. 1982).

Today, microcomputers are powerful enough to act as file servers, and CAI can be delivered either through an integrated learning system or as stand-alone software. Typical CAI software provides text and multiple-choice questions or problems to students, offers immediate feedback, notes incorrect responses, summarizes students' performance, and generates exercises for worksheets and tests. CAI typically presents tasks for which there is one (and only one) correct answer; it can evaluate simple numeric or very simple alphabetic responses, but it cannot evaluate complex student responses.

Integrated learning systems (ILSs) are networked CAI systems that manage individualized instruction in core curriculum areas (mathematics, science, language arts, reading, writing). ILSs differ from most stand-alone CAI in their use of a network (i.e., computer terminals are connected to a central computer) and in their more extensive student record-keeping capabilities. The systems are sold as packages, incorporating both the hardware and software for setting up a computer lab.

ILSs are typically sold in sets of 30 workstations, with an average cost of about $125,000. Major producers include Josten's Learning Corporation, WICAT Systems, and CCC (founded by Patrick Suppes). About 10,000 ILSs are in use in U.S. schools, most of them purchased with funds from the ESEA Chapter 1 program for at-risk students (Mageau 1990).

The instructional software within ILSs is typically conventional CAI: instruction is organized into discrete content areas (mathematics, reading, etc.) and requires simple responses from students. ILS developers have also made a point of developing systems that tie into the major basal textbooks. Mageau (1990) notes that the systems "can correlate almost objective by objective to a district's K-8... language arts, reading, math, and even science curricula." Users of ILSs enjoy the advantage of having one coordinated system, making it easy for students to use a large selection of software.

A new trend in integrated learning systems is represented by *ClassWorks*, developed by Computer Networking Specialists. *ClassWorks* offers the school access to whatever variety of third-party software the teachers select, along with all the instructional management features associated with an ILS (Mageau 1990).

CAI in general, and integrated learning systems in particular, have found a niche in America's schools by fitting into existing school structures (Newman 1990a). Cohen (1988) describes these structures as follows:

- Most instruction occurs in groups of 25 to 35 students in small segments from 45 to 50 minutes long.

- Instruction is usually either whole-class or completely individual.

- Instruction is teacher dominated, with teachers doing most of the talking and student talk confined largely to brief answers to teacher questions.

- When students work on their own, they complete handouts devised or selected by the teacher. Students have little responsibility for selecting goals or deadlines and little chance to explore issues in depth. Most responses are brief.

- Knowledge is represented as mastery of isolated bits of information and discrete skills.

Many features of tutorial CAI are consistent with the traditional classroom described by Cohen. Tutorial CAI provides a one-way (computer to student) transmission of knowledge; it presents information and the student is expected to learn the information presented. Much CAI software presents information in a single curriculum area (e.g., arithmetic or vocabulary) and uses brief exercises that can easily be accommodated within the typical 50-minute academic period. CAI is designed for use by a single student and can be accommodated into a regular class schedule if computers are placed in a laboratory into which various whole classes are scheduled.

Basic skills (such as the ability to add or spell) lend themselves to drill-and-practice activities, and CAI, with its ability to generate exercises (e.g., mathematics problems or vocabulary words) is well suited to providing extensive drill and practice in basic skills. Students at risk of academic failure—often seen as lacking in basic skills and therefore unable to acquire advanced thinking skills—become logical candidates for CAI drill-and-practice instruction. Recent research and thinking on the needs of disadvantaged students stress a different need, however (see Knapp & Turnbull 1990; Means, Knapp & Chelemer 1991). Disadvantaged students need the opportunity to acquire advanced thinking skills and can acquire basic skills within the context of complex, meaningful problems. This latter approach to instruction, which is stressed in education reform, has not been well served by traditional CAI.

Intelligent Computer-Assisted Instruction—Intelligent computer-assisted instruction (ICAI, also known as intelligent tutoring systems or ITSs) grew out of generative computer-assisted instruction. Programs that generated problems and tasks in arithmetic and vocabulary learning eventually were designed to select problems at a difficulty level appropriate for individual students (Suppes 1980). These adaptive systems (i.e., adapting problems to the student's learning level) were based on summaries of a student's performance on earlier tasks, however, rather than on representations of the student's knowledge of the subject matter (Sleeman & Brown 1982). The truly intelligent systems that followed were able to present problems based on models of the student's knowledge, to solve problems themselves, and to diagnose and explain student capabilities.

Historically, ICAI systems have been developed in more mathematically oriented domains—arithmetic, algebra, programming—and have been more experimental in nature than has conventional CAI. Although ICAI is an area of active research projects, ICAI programs in the schools are not widespread. ICAI tends to call for more meaningful interactions than traditional CAI and tends to deal with more complex subject matter. ICAI's focus on modeling student knowledge lends itself to applications in teaching advanced thinking skills. ICAI has not been used extensively with disadvantaged students (traditional targets for basic skills instruction).

One intelligent tutoring system, *Geometry Tutor*, provides students with instruction in planning and problem solving to prove theorems in geometry (Office of Technology Assessment 1988). *Geometry Tutor* comprises an expert system containing knowledge of how to construct geometry proofs, a tutor to teach students strategies and to identify their errors, and an interface to let students communicate with the computer. *Geometry Tutor* monitors students as they try to prove theorems, instructing and guiding them throughout the problem-solving process (Anderson et al. 1985). Schofield, Evans-Rhodes, and Huber (1989) studied the implementation of *Geometry Tutor* in a public high school and found changes in the behavior of teachers and students using this system: teachers spent more time with students having problems, collaborated more with students, and based more of a student's grade on effort; students increased their level of effort and were more involved in the academic tasks. Thus, ICAI can be implemented in ways that support the kind of learning that education reformers advocate. Although most of these applications control instructional content, they can be used within a broader instructional framework that stresses joint work with the automated tutor.

Distance-Learning with One-Way Transmission

As with computer-based instruction, the first applications of distance-learning were tutorial in nature. The term *distance-learning* is used to describe the delivery of instruction from a single site to multiple remote sites. In the early part of this century, film and radio were the distance-learning methods used to instruct students (Cuban 1986). As technologies have become more sophisticated and diffuse, many other methods and delivery systems have been incorporated. One-way video technology (broadcast, cable, and videotape) has been widely used as an instructional medium and as a vehicle for distance-learning in both homes and schools. (Newer, interactive forms of distance-learning are discussed later in this chapter as examples of educational uses of communication technology.)

Technology was used in the 1950s in part to help alleviate a lack of qualified teachers. In one well-known example, the school district in Hagerstown, Maryland, provided closed-circuit television programming in nearly all core curriculum areas to all of its schools. The courses were taught live from six studios and represented an attempt to change the way schooling took place in the district (Rockman 1991). Although the actual instruction tended to be traditional, a strength of those programs was that they brought qualified instructors to an audience of students who would not otherwise have had access to them.

In addition to bringing students instructional content they could not receive otherwise, distance-learning can provide teachers with models of new ways to teach. During the "new math" era of the 1960s, educators at the University of Wisconsin developed *Patterns in Arithmetic*, a program that included, in addition to workbooks, television lessons broadcast to elementary school classes. Use of the program was high initially but subsided as teachers learned the content and began to provide instruction in new math themselves (Rockman 1991). This unintended outcome suggests that teachers can internalize content and teaching techniques displayed through distance-learning technology.

Most early uses of instructional television featured conventional, lecture-based approaches to instruction, recreating the basic elements of the traditional classroom. In the 1970s, a new breed of instructional programming appeared. Following the widespread popularity and success of Children's Television Workshop's *Sesame Street*, a host of similar programs were produced for home and school viewing (Johnston 1987). These programs made rich use of the visual and auditory capabilities of video, combining teaching with entertainment as a way to gain and maintain the attention of the learner, while getting the information across in interesting and innovative ways. Currently, educators and parents have a broad diversity of programs from which to choose. Instructional television programming is limited in being one-way communication, but the production values and creativity of these presentations can be very high, reflecting a level of resources that no single teacher could command.

In the past, incompatibility between broadcast schedules and school timetables was a major impediment to the use of instructional television, but current technology has overcome this difficulty: programming can be received and videotaped for use at any convenient time. Instructional programming can be communicated over cable television, broadcast television, or satellite.

The Public Broadcasting Service (PBS) offers educational video programming in mathematics, reading, social science, and other content areas. Series such as *Square One TV*, *Reading Rainbow*, *Ghostwriter*, and *Voyage of the Mimi* have proved to be immensely popular with children.

Cable television is another source of instructional programming, which is typically noninteractive and designed to fit specific academic content areas. Millions of homes receive educational broadcasts from The Learning Channel, The Discovery Channel, and other instructional sources (Douglas & Bransford 1991).

A more recent trend in educational television is the transmission of educational news broadcasts. *CNN Newsroom* and *Channel One* offer news and current events information. *CNN Newsroom* is broadcast week nights without commercials on Cable News Network for use with students in grades 6-12; it contains news and current events and is meant to be videotaped during the night and used in the following day's classes. In contrast, Whittle Communications' controversial *Channel One*, with an audience of over 6 million students, broadcasts not only news but also commercial advertising (Sheekey & Douglas 1991).

Educational video, used thoughtfully, can contribute to education reform goals, insofar as it integrates various subject matter areas—e.g., history, archaeology, research methods, art, reading, literature, and mathematics—and challenges students to understand the complex relationships that exist among various domains. Moreover, research on instructional television has demonstrated positive effects of viewing upon learning in a variety of domains, such as children's math problem solving (research on *Square One TV*, Hall, Esty & Fisch 1990) and social attitudes (research on *Freestyle,* Johnston & Ettma 1986). A consistent finding within the research is that the potential benefits associated with instructional programming are most likely to be realized within settings where teachers (or parents) assist young viewers in making sense of what they see. Students get more out of watching instructional television when teachers set the stage for what they will watch and follow up with discussion, probing questions, and relevant activities (Bryant, Alexander & Brown 1983; Johnston & Ettma 1986).

Videodiscs

Videodisc technology combines the features of video with the flexibility of a computer. Videodisc technology can be used in either a tutorial or an exploratory fashion (the latter type of video applications is discussed later). Used alone, a videodisc player enables the user to access and sequence visual images (still and motion) and accompanying audio tracks in a nonlinear and selective manner. Used in combination with appropriate hardware and software, videodisc technology may be used as an individualized, interactive learning tool, integrating visual and auditory information with electronic text. Like many other instructional technologies reviewed in this chapter, a videodisc system lends itself to an array of instructional activities and approaches, from teachers creating their own customized presentations to students exploring a topic by accessing the information on a videodisc.

In some states, notably Texas, videodiscs are being used for tutorial instruction by either supplementing or, in some cases, supplanting textbooks. Optical Data Corporation's *Windows on Science* videodisc and associated print materials have been adopted by at least 65 percent of the schools in Texas (Soloway 1991). Using videodisc images, teachers can demonstrate science information to their students. Additionally, individual students or groups of students can review material on the machine. Teachers can present lessons by picking video clips and still photographs from a set of videodiscs approved by the state as a textbook.

The merging of video and computer technology, and the flexibility this affords, make videodisc technology a potentially powerful vehicle for instruction, especially in areas where visual and auditory information are essential to understanding.

Disadvantages cited for videodisc technology include the need for fairly expensive equipment, lack of teacher facility with the technology, and nonstandardized videodisc equipment (Yoder 1991). Because of the high cost and the high level of technical facility previously associated with the production and utilization of videodisc programs, most videodisc applications have been targeted for use within business and industry. However, recent technological developments are making videodisc technology more cost effective, more compatible with standard computer systems, and much easier to use (e.g., barcode readers and symbols within a text can simplify access to relevant video). In addition, other technological innovations, such as CD-ROM, offer advantages similar to videodisc (e.g., random access to graphics, sounds, text) in a relatively inexpensive and easy-to-use format. These advances are likely to increase the use of videodisc and related technologies within the educational arena.

Summary

Technologies for tutorial learning typically use a transmission rather than constructivist model of instruction. For this reason, although they have found their place in education and have the greatest rate of adoption within schools thus far, they are unlikely to serve as a catalyst for restructuring education. The focus of drill-and-practice CAI on basic skills allows little room for the presentation of complex tasks, multistep problems, or collaborative learning. ICAI, on the other hand, has the potential to deal with complex domains, to provide models of higher-order thinking, and to probe students' understanding, but has seldom been well integrated into a school's mainstream curriculum. One-way video technologies can be very motivating but are nearly always viewed as enrichment and have not instigated fundamental changes within schools.

Technologies for Exploratory Learning

Exploratory uses of instructional technology allow students to direct their own learning. Through the process of discovery, or guided discovery, the student learns facts, concepts, and procedures. In this section, we describe three broad types of technology used for exploratory learning: computer-based information retrieval systems (e.g., electronic databases), microworlds (including microcomputer-based labs and simulations), and interactive video. Although different in form and application, each of these uses of instructional technology provides a context in which the student may access, discover, and construct knowledge through a self-directed learning process. Exploratory uses of technology tend to deal with complex learning activities. Such uses of technology are very congruent with the goals of education reform.

Electronic Databases

Electronic reference works provide students with a way to access large bodies of information quickly and in a self-selected manner. In addition to serving as information retrieval systems, electronic databases can provide students with capabilities for organizing and manipulating data that they have accessed or entered. Within the physical and social sciences, databases can be used to explore and test the relationships between variables within complex systems. Some electronic reference works and databases incorporate graphics and/or sound, providing students with additional sources of information.

Electronic databases and references are developing at a dizzying speed. Some of these, such as Sony's *Data Discman* or Franklin's *World Almanac*, are—at an elementary level—beginning to fulfill Alan Kay's vision of a *dynabook*—a powerful, hand-held computer that will allow students to access a wide array of information (Gillingham 1991). The *Data Discman* is a hand-held compact disc player that can read "books" published on compact disc. Each compact disc can hold up to 100,000 pages of text—enough for encyclopedias of all types. Currently available is an abridged *Encyclopaedia Britannica*, a health encyclopedia, and a comprehensive language translator. Although not yet widely in use, the *Data Discman* could become a compact, economical machine for knowledge retrieval. In a similar vein, Franklin Electronic Publishers is planning to introduce a hand-held, electronic version of *The World Almanac and Book of Facts*.

All of this hand-held power does have a potential disadvantage: it is easy to imagine students getting lost in the myriad of facts available to them at the touch of a button. It should be remembered that access to information is great, but true intellectual capability comes from having a conceptual framework within which to assimilate that information. Teachers need to take an active role to make sure that students have the conceptual structures needed to profit from the reference information.

Computer-Based Exploratory Applications

Microcomputer-based labs and microworlds have proven to be effective contexts for learning in mathematics and the physical and social sciences. Microcomputer-based labs put the tools of the scientist at the students' disposal, enabling them to engage in scientific inquiry with real-life phenomena. Simulations create self-enclosed microworlds that mimic real-life phenomena, allowing students to explore and manipulate complex systems. Simulations are available for a wide variety of subject areas, including biology, genetics, geology, chemistry, physics, environmentalism, social studies, economics, and mathematics. Some simulations are multidisciplinary, allowing students to develop and apply their knowledge in a variety of subject areas. The examples that follow provide an exemplary, but by no means exhaustive, overview of the range of software supporting inquiry-based learning through interaction with microworlds.

Microcomputer-based laboratories (MBLs) allow students to explore real-life, real-time phenomena. Typically, MBLs consist of measurement equipment or sensors connecting a computer and the environment. The equipment (commonly referred to as probeware) measures physical phenomena, such as sound, light, or temperature, and records data that can be displayed as it is being recorded, or saved and analyzed at a later date. This real-time measurement with real-time display capabilities offers students an opportunity to better understand the connection between a phenomenon and its graphic or mathematical representations (Office of Technology Assessment 1988). Rather than fostering the rote memorization of unconnected facts, MBLs facilitate the direct observation of, and inquiry into, scientific phenomena. Students utilize the tools of the scientist to engage in the processes of hypothesis testing, data collection, and data analyses. (The way in which MBLs are used in classrooms is described in more detail in Chapter III.)

One of the earliest and best known examples of computer-based exploratory learning is the use of LOGO, a computer language developed in the 1970s by Seymour Papert and his colleagues at the MIT Artificial Intelligence Laboratory. LOGO was specifically designed as a programming language to facilitate the acquisition of critical thinking and mathematical problem-solving skills in learners of all ages. In many schools across the country and around the world, LOGO, in its various incarnations, has been used by students to create microworlds in which mathematical and physical principles are tested and explored.

In one of its simplest forms, LOGO can be used by young children to create designs through programming the movements of a "turtle" on the computer screen. In the process of building upon simple commands to get the turtle to "draw" a variety of shapes, children discover and construct knowledge regarding geometrical concepts. In another, more advanced application, students learn the laws of physics through programming the movement of objects (such as dynaturtles) that simulate Newton's laws of motion. Concepts needed to understand these laws (velocity, acceleration, and position) are discovered, explored, and tested as students use simple commands to manipulate the objects within this microworld.

LOGOWriter provides students with the word-processing, graphics, and animation capabilities to create their own animated games and stories. With LegoLOGO, students use construction materials (Lego building blocks, pulleys, gears, motors), sensors (temperature, light, and sound), and the LOGO programming language to design, produce, and control real objects in the physical world. Taking on the roles of inventors and engineers, students have used LegoLOGO to build and operate mechanical devices (such as robots, cars, and moving sculptures), as well as whole environments (such as model cities). LOGO can serve as a project-based vehicle for multidisciplinary learning, as when students use LegoLOGO to create their own version of Willy Wonka's Chocolate Factory, or use LOGOWriter to create animated narratives on historical events. In providing students with the tools for creating their own microworlds, LOGO offers a meaningful context for learning about the design process as well as discovering complex scientific and mathematical concepts.

Although much of the exploratory computer software available concerns science phenomena, there is also a growing body of social science software that allows students to explore decision-making and complex relationships in sociopolitical spheres (Office of Technology Assessment 1988). Two rather new and popular software programs, *SimCity* and *SimEarth*, allow users to act as civic or world leaders, manipulating variables to maintain the system. In the course of building and managing simulated cities or planets, students encounter a range of problems and issues (political, economic, environmental) that lead to learning and problem solving across interrelated domains.

The immensely popular *Where in the World Is Carmen Sandiego?* and related programs in the series require students to track a fugitive by looking for clues and gathering information not only from the software but from outside reference sources, to make predictions, and to confirm hypotheses (Zorfass 1991). In addition to teaching geography, by requiring students to explore, experiment, evaluate, and revise, these self-contained worlds facilitate student collaboration in the higher-order thinking skills of deduction, inference, synthesis, and evaluation.

Stanley Pogrow of the University of Arizona designed the *Higher Order Thinking Skills* (HOTS) program to teach disadvantaged students advanced thinking skills (Office of Technology Assessment 1988). This program uses a combination of teacher activities and computer software to promote the development of metacognition, inference, generalizing, and synthesis (Pogrow 1990). In a typical unit, students spend one period using a computer simulation to study the dynamics of a balloon in flight. The next day, the teacher asks students to describe the effects of fuel, wind direction, terrain, and the balloon's capabilities on its movement. Students are asked to describe the strategies they used in controlling the balloon. Those whose balloons crashed are asked to describe their strategies and what happened. After a set of alternative strategies are elicited, they are tried out and tested with the simulation.

Pogrow (1990) reports that the HOTS program is used in more than 300 sites in 21 states; it is used mainly within Chapter 1 programs and its success supports the argument that students who have been labeled "at risk" can accomplish much more than they do in conventional classrooms if they are appropriately challenged. Research on the HOTS program has shown that students make greater-than-average gains in their standardized reading and math scores (Office of Technology Assessment 1988). Pogrow (1990) reported to the National Diffusion Network that HOTS students gained nearly twice as much on measures of reading and math as did Chapter 1 students nationally.

Video Exploratory Applications

Video exploratory applications support higher-order thinking by presenting complex, authentic tasks that transcend the boundaries of academic disciplines. Students engaged in video exploration may learn how to solve novel problems requiring several steps and involving several disciplines (e.g., arithmetic, geography, and reading). Recent theory and research suggest that children who learn with difficulty may particularly benefit from this kind of instruction with its focus on conceptual understanding and solving novel problems (Sutton 1991).

The Cognition and Technology Group (1991) at Vanderbilt University has designed a series of video adventures, known as the *Adventures of Jasper Woodbury*, requiring mathematical reasoning to solve complex problems in trip planning, probability and statistics, and geometry. Videos 17 to 20 minutes in length provide natural contexts for learning mathematics as well as geography, history, and science. Each video ends with a challenge, rather than a resolution. The information to solve the problem is embedded within the video, which can be reviewed and studied to pick out relevant facts.

The Cognition and Technology Group has based its design of these episodes on a set of principles drawn from research on cognition and instruction. These researchers argue that by being video based, the learning experience is more motivating and allows for more complex problems than could be presented in a written or audio-only medium. Motivation and comprehension are further heightened through use of a narrative format, that is, a story providing a realistic context and a familiar structure for the problems presented. The narrative format provides for the introduction of other subject matter topics; for example, the skill of map reading is used in an episode dealing with trip planning, thus providing links to geography and navigation. The learning format is generative; the stories in the *Jasper* series must be completed with a resolution provided by the students. Generating this resolution requires solving a complex mathematics problem. This is motivating and allows students to participate actively in the learning process. Data needed to solve the problem are embedded in the story itself, just as in other good mystery stories. The videos are created in pairs of related adventures so that students can transfer any mathematics or reasoning concepts learned in one video context to new contexts.

The *Jasper* videos are being designed to be available through a variety of media: videotape, videodisc, and in conjunction with hypermedia (Cognition and Technology Group 1991). In the hypermedia version, students can engage in basic skills practice, change parameters of the original problem to generate an analogous problem (new locations, goals, etc.), and explore related mini-adventures. The materials are being tried out and evaluated in 52 classrooms in nine states.

An earlier major exploratory video project, *Palenque*, consists of a videodisc and software that allow students to explore a Mayan ruin in southern Mexico. Begun at the Bank Street College of Education in 1985, *Palenque* was developed as a prototype demonstration of digital video interactive (DVI) technology. Slides, film, video, graphics, text, sound effects, and audio narration are all integrated on an optical videodisc. Students use a joystick to take user-directed simulated journeys through a rain forest or a "museum" database of the ancient Mayan site at Palenque. The *Palenque* materials are designed to be student directed rather than dependent on a teacher's instructional sequence and objectives—the materials foster browsing that will be both informative and enjoyable. Students are given simulated travel tools, such as a camera, photo album, and compass. When they want to know more about something they are seeing, they can click on a button and get commentary from a simulated 8-year-old Mayan specialist (Soloway 1991; Wilson & Tally 1991).

Other examples of exploratory video include *GTV*, a multimedia, video-based geography program produced by LucasFilms and National Geographic; *Animal Pathfinders*, an exploratory program focusing on animal migration (with footage from the *Nova* television series); and *Civil War Interactive*, a multimedia work based on the popular public television series by Ken Burns.

Summary

These exploratory applications can support the kind of student learning that is the goal of education reform. They can present complex, authentic tasks, engage students in active problem solving, require utilization and synthesis of knowledge from a variety of domains, and provide a context for collaborative learning activities.

There are, however, significant practical limitations, to many of these applications. First, there is the issue of scarcity—complex simulations and exploratory videos are expensive to develop, hence they are few. The problem is made worse by the fragmentation of the American education market, with its decentralized buying decisions and wide variation in curricula. Technology application developers have little hope of being able to match the curriculum of enough schools well enough to have a broad market base (Levin & Meister 1985). Without such a broad base, they see little hope of recapturing a major investment. From the teacher's standpoint, these exciting and imaginative applications are fine for enrichment but don't match the core curriculum. Hence, they may find a home in the "margins" of education but don't really transform the core. Finally, exploratory applications have a relatively short "shelf life." Once students learn how to solve, complete, or engage in the complex tasks required by the simulation or video, they are ready to move on to something else.

One factor that may change the economics of producing multimedia educational materials is the potential for a much larger home-use market. These materials are sufficiently entertaining that the home market is a feasible primary or secondary target. *Palenque*, in fact, was designed for home use by families with children 8 to 14 years old. Another multimedia technology being developed for home use is Commodore Dynamic Total Vision (CDTV), a hybrid television, personal computer, compact disc technology system, which combines an optical disc player with a computer. Priced at under $1,000, CDTV hooks up to a standard television and allows control of sound, animation, text, graphics, and quarter-screen full-motion video. The fast pace of multimedia technology development for home use with the expected drop in technology prices may prove to be a catalyst for major investments in materials that have both educational and entertainment value.

Technology as Applications

One of the most significant shifts in the way that technology is being used in education today is toward greater use of computers and other devices as *tools* in the learning process rather than as instructional delivery devices. Such uses mirror the ways in which technology is used in the workplace and at home. Word processing, desktop publishing, database and spreadsheet applications, and drawing, painting, and graphing programs are examples of technology tools. Whenever students compose using a word processor, spell check their composition, use an on-screen calculator or graphing program, manipulate data in a spreadsheet, look up information in a database, or "publish" a classroom newspaper, they are using computers as tools. Video and audiotaping and editing equipment are other tools finding their way into schools.

Using technology as tools solves a major problem that frequently arises in the use of technology for tutorial or exploratory uses—that of the technology's curriculum not being consistent with the teacher's curriculum. Often, tutorial or exploratory products that are interesting in their own right do not have a place in a given school's course of study. In contrast, when technology is used as a tool, the teacher can still control the curriculum and the instructional strategy. The technology merely provides students with aids for studying that content or practicing those skills. Tool products can be applied in a variety of curricular activities—word processors for writing and revising assignments, graphing programs for mathematics instruction, desktop publishing systems for producing newspapers, and hypermedia systems for development of one's own study materials.

Technology tools are designed to facilitate educational and work-related tasks. They are flexible, lending themselves to a wide variety of activities across the grade levels and throughout the curriculum. From an education reform perspective, this flexibility is both a strength and a weakness. Whether technology tools are applied in ways that promote traditional instruction or education reform is dependent on the perspective, skills, and practices of the classroom teacher.

Word Processing and Related Applications

The most frequently used computer-based tool in U.S. education today is word processing software. When the first personal computers began to appear in the early 1970s, they were quickly followed by word processing software modeled after the early text editing programs. During the 1980s there was an explosion of microcomputers, and word processing applications became easier to learn and use. Both because facility with this software will assist students in higher education and work and because its support for revisions was expected to encourage students to edit their own work, teachers soon began experimenting with having students use word processing software for their compositions.

Over the past decade, a broad range of word-processing software has become available for educational use, covering virtually every grade level. Word processors *may* support higher-order thinking by allowing students to attend to the composing process, focusing more on ideas and ways to communicate them than on the mechanics of spelling and punctuation. With word processing software, students can easily review and revise their compositions, highlight key ideas, rearrange sentences or paragraphs to flow more logically, and try out alternative sentences or words to communicate their ideas better. The mechanics of spelling can be dealt with separately, assisted by a spell checker.

The authenticity of writing tasks is enhanced when students are given the opportunity to produce professional-looking documents, which can readily be shared with others. Standard word-processing software (which includes typestyle choices and formatting options), when used in conjunction with printers, provides students with a flexible tool for creating polished documents. Desktop publishing tools further enhance this capability. Many teachers have found this aspect of computer-supported writing to be tremendously motivating for students. In addition to taking personal pride in the look of their products, students are eager to share their work with others. Their writing skills develop within the context of meaningful activities, as they become increasingly aware of audience concerns and learn to plan and revise their texts more carefully.

More recent technology developments add to the tools that students can use to support writing and editing processes. For example, word processors incorporating speech synthesis "read back" what the student has written, allowing beginning writers to explore the relationship between sounds and written symbols (Borg 1985; Rosegrant 1986). Instructionally enhanced word processors offer cognitive support, in the form of questions, prompts, and/or suggestions, for compositional tasks that are particularly difficult for many students, such as the planning (Rubin & Bruce 1985) and revision of text (Daiute 1986). Grammar analysis programs, electronic thesauri, integrated software packages, and desktop publishing software are additional examples of tools that may serve to support and extend students' developing capabilities as writers.

Pea and Kurland (1987) see the next step in writing technologies as software that acts as critic, writing expert, teacher, audience, or collaborator. However, as Zorfass (1991) points out, it is the teacher, not the technology, who designs the context within which students will learn and practice their writing skills. Word processing software in and of itself does not facilitate higher-order thinking, revision, or collaboration unless the teacher creates a structure for doing so.

Hypermedia Tools

In addition to the new electronic databases and references discussed in the section on exploratory technologies, classrooms are starting to develop their own electronic reference and learning tools using *hypermedia*. Hypermedia consists of a database of information structured as nodes or frames, specified links between these nodes that allow for rapid movement through the information, and a user interface. Hypermedia can be used for (1) exploring a large database of information, (2) accessing elaborations on core information, or (3) building a database (Duffy & Knuth 1989). Although hypermedia can provide didactic instruction (by containing instructive text and graphics and tutorials) and exploratory learning (through simulations), in this discussion we stress its uses as a tool, either as a reference source for knowledge and information or as a tool for storing and structuring information to be accessed by others.

The most widely available hypermedia system is *HyperCard*, which has been distributed free by Apple Computer with its Macintosh computer systems. *HyperCard* stacks can contain still and animated graphics, text, and sound; they have been used for database management, demonstrations, and instruction. Given the ease of use of *HyperCard*, students and educators can create personal database stacks, educational simulation stacks, and tutorial stacks. With *QuickTime*, a multimedia integration package for the Macintosh, students and teachers can add video footage to their products.

In the Computer-Supported Intentional Learning Environments (CSILE) project, students use hypermedia to write, illustrate, read, and comment on material as they study science, history, and social studies. The system is used collaboratively, with students able to access each other's work and comment on it. Commenters may provide additional information, questions, or commendations. The author of the node being commented on is notified by the system, setting the stage for an electronic interchange concerning the content (Scardamalia, Bereiter, McLean, Swallow & Woodruff 1989).

In another project involving hypermedia, Discover Rochester, disadvantaged middle school students created a hypermedia exhibit, incorporating text, audio, graphics, maps, and music, describing their city for the Rochester Museum and Science Center. To gather material for the exhibit, the students conducted research on the city's weather, industry, culture, and economics. They worked in libraries and archives, performed observations in the field, interviewed people by telephone and face-to-face, and conducted experiments. Students learned to use a variety of computer software in order to best present their findings, and carefully crafted and revised their presentation (Collins, Hawkins & Carver 1991). Teachers in the Rochester project integrated computer tools, such as *MacPaint, MacWrite, CricketGraph,* and *HyperCard,* into the software environment to create a natural work environment, where tools for exploring real-world topics were an "invisible" part of the work space. Multiple experiences in using these tools in their research are designed to help students learn to select the appropriate tool for any stage of an investigation, without teacher guidance.

Hypermedia, insofar as it allows the creation of personal education applications, has the potential to circumvent the problems of "hard-wired" information retrieval systems (such as CD-ROM). If students themselves create or manipulate data in hypermedia (i.e., control the creation and linking of nodes or cards in hyperstacks), they should have better conceptual maps of the information. Research by Richard Lehrer (1992) and others supports this claim. Lehrer finds that students using hypermedia develop and retain more elaborated concepts, chiefly for those areas in which they themselves developed materials (personal communication). Hypermedia may be less useful for the person accessing information compiled by others. Students will not learn much from hypermedia if they get lost in a myriad of facts and information, lose track of where they are within the hypermedia, and do not understand the links created by another hypermedia author. Developers are working on tools to assist users in "navigating" through hypermedia stacks.

Video Production

With the increasing affordability and popularity of video cassette recorders and hand-held video cameras, this technology is finding its way into more and more schools. Many of the high-level planning and communication issues that enter into the process of composing written text have their analogs in designing video reports. Teachers are finding video equipment to be highly motivating and educationally valuable when used within a context that promotes study and analysis of socially important themes.

With more sophisticated technology, students can produce compositions combining computer text, video, and audio media. The *MultiMedia Works* Club (Pea 1991) is an example of an application that promotes an innovative and restructured conception of education, taking learning beyond the school walls. The technology used in the club, *MultiMedia Works,* is based on a film-making metaphor and allows students to combine text, video, computer graphics, and sound to compose, in effect, multimedia movies (Soloway 1991). The *MultiMedia Works* Club was held after school for students and teachers from a high-poverty area. The students selected topics, collected video and audio information in the field, assembled relevant media clips for their compositions, collaboratively produced their compositions, allowed their work to be critiqued, revised their work, and presented their compositions to others (Pea 1991; Allen 1991). Pea (1991) noted that "students learned to employ critical thinking skills while conducting their own discussions to analyze the media they had collected, focus on their chosen topic, and then select and logically organize the media to communicate their ideas".

Summary

Used well, technology applications can support higher-order thinking by engaging students in authentic, complex tasks within collaborative learning contexts. (The kinds of support provided by technology are discussed in more details in Chapter III.) Moreover, the projects described above have made it clear that projects using technology applications to support advanced skills can be successful with disadvantaged students.

Word processors facilitate the process of writing as a complex task. Both by facilitating the revision process and by handling mechanical aspects of writing, this technology can help focus attention on higher-level issues of content and organization. Use of this technology within a collaborative learning format appears particularly promising for providing students with modeling of the metacognitive skills involved in writing and editing.

Proponents of hypermedia argue that its nonlinear format, allowing students access to vast amounts of information with complex links to other information, promotes "rich" learning (Duffy & Knuth 1989). Although intriguing, these claims are still speculative. The clear advantage to hypermedia systems is their invitation to students to enter and manipulate information—copy it, modify or analyze it, or link it to other nodes. Thus, the technology invites active processing on the part of users. Additionally, hypermedia databases can be developed collaboratively by groups of students interested in particular information, subjects, or topics. Used in this way, hypermedia encourages students to act as researchers and to figure out how to organize the fruits of their research in a way that will be easy to use and interesting for others to explore.

Multimedia application systems redefine the teaching learning process and model the kind of education reform possible with new technologies. The tasks in which the students engage—library research, scanning media, talking to experts, recording information, writing or otherwise producing compositions—reflect the kinds of tasks in which they will continue to engage throughout their careers. The tasks are authentic and multidisciplinary. Additionally, students who use multimedia tools are active learners: choosing composition topics, doing fieldwork, and, at times, teaching the teachers. Students work collaboratively, not only with each other, but with researchers and teachers. Finally, given the complex nature of producing multimedia compositions, heterogeneous student groups function well; students with skills in different areas (e.g., videography, script writing, editing) complement each other and teach and learn from one another.

Technologies for Communication

By communication applications we mean those educational uses that allow students or teachers at different sites to send and receive written, vocal, or visual information. These communications may come over telephone lines, through computers and modems, via voice or audiographic communication, or through satellite or other technologies. One-way transmission of information was discussed earlier, as a tutorial use of technology. Here we focus on technology uses that are interactive, with both parties providing information and shaping the nature of the exchange.

Interactive communication technologies in common use today include two-way text-based (e.g., computer networks), two-way audio (e.g., telephone, cellular telephone), two-way video/two-way audio (e.g., fiber optic), and one-way video/two-way audio (hybrid) systems. Two-way video/two-way audio systems are still rare, but on the increase.

Computer Networks

A relatively inexpensive technology, computer networking increasingly is being used in classrooms across the nation. These networks allow computers to send and receive information to and from other geographic sites. Harasim (1990) identifies a number of advantages shared by these on-line systems. Networks allow many students/teachers to communicate with many other students/teachers, hence encouraging collaboration and active participation on the part of learners. Freeing learning from the constraint of geographic location, networks let learners and teachers participate in the education experience without regard to their physical location. Likewise, networks free learning from the constraints of time: students and teachers can "log on" to networks at times that are most convenient for them. Participants need not be confined to traditional school-day hours and can take time in reviewing information presented on the network before responding, thus allowing for more thoughtful responses. Given the text-based nature of networks, many believe that they encourage verbal communication, writing skills, and the articulation of ideas. Finally, networks are computer-based, hence they tap into record-keeping and management functions that might be costly in non-technology-based communication.

Various networks for children or for education have been established (e.g., Kids Network and FrEdMail). Networks are being used for "learning circles" or for innovative writing applications. Benefits of networks include collaborative learning and greater exposure to national or global perspectives. The National Geographic Society in association with the National Science Foundation sponsors the Kids Network (developed by the Technical Education Research Center, or TERC), on which students can electronically send data they have collected to other schools around the United States. Scientists produce a national report utilizing the students' data, and they make themselves available, via electronic mail, to answer students' questions (Heller

1991). (Interactions on this network are described in greater detail in Chapter III.) Along similar lines, NASA's SpaceLink program connects students with astronauts and scientists.

Another model of collaborative learning uses networks to allow students at diverse sites to share activities and ideas and learn from each other. AT&T's Long Distance Learning Network has been used to promote "learning circles," electronic communities composed of about eight classrooms each whose students and teachers collaborate on relevant educational projects (Riel 1990c). These projects come from within the classrooms' curricula and allow students actively to research, locate, and share knowledge with students and teachers at the other sites. Riel (1990b) noted that the "learning circle" requires collaborative work among the students, with students taking on the role of teacher and participating actively in the learning process. The circles benefit teachers as well by reducing their isolation from colleagues, as will be discussed in Chapter IV.

Similar network-based educational experiences have been reported for the FrEdMail network (Levin, Waugh, Kim, & Miyake 1990). Electronic communication can start when someone proposes an idea on the network. Others respond favorably to the idea, or the idea dies away. If there is favorable response, the interested individuals exchange electronic mail, and the idea's proponent sets up a conference. Levin, Kim, and Riel (1990) found that successful networks exhibited at least four of the following five features:

- Students and teachers, even though they were not in the same location, shared an interest in the educational projects;

- Educational projects were well specified;

- Sites had easy access to a reliable computer network;

- Students and teachers had a sense of responsibility to the project or the network community; and

- Strong leadership and a final evaluation of the project were provided.

Not all networking experiences need be as elaborate as those reported above. Students can use networks merely to communicate with other students or with adults, and these simpler communications may hold educational benefits. Griffin and Cole (1987) described innovative applications of communications technology in their research with minority students. An international exchange in real time between students in San Diego, California, and students in Pistoia, Italy, resulted in the American students' identifying some similarities between the Italian and Spanish languages (some of the students were bilingual) and learning concretely about the notion of time zones. Another group of students used the network to write "rap" to university researchers in real time.

Thinking and composition skills that were not apparent in much of their school work became evident when students were engaged in a task that was meaningful to them. Barriers created by differences in age and cultural group were lessened when communicating over a network.

Videotapes

Not all communication technologies involve a computer and modem. Alternative communication technologies may be quite economical, small–scale, and under considerable student and teacher control. VideoPals, a program founded in 1990, promotes video pen pals. Classes join the service and are matched with an appropriate class in another part of the world. The U.S. class makes a videotape, sends it to VideoPals for conversion to the foreign video standard (if different from the U.S. standard), and mails the converted tape to the videopal class. After viewing the video, the foreign class creates a video and sends it to the U.S. class. Richard Ray, the founder of the program, reports that interest is maintained when the videos point out differences between the two classes/communities, have visual or emotional impact, and require student research and script writing.

Interactive Learning at a Distance

Distance-learning systems supporting one-way transmission have been discussed earlier in this chapter as a technology for tutorial instruction. Here, we discuss the more interactive forms of distance-learning made possible when audio and visual signals can travel in both directions.

Two-Way Video/Two-Way Audio—Systems that provide both visual and auditory communication allow the maximum amount of interactivity between teachers and students. These two-way video/two-way audio systems provide monitors, cameras, and microphones at the teacher's and multiple students' sites. The teacher can see and hear the students; students can see and hear the teacher and can see and hear each other. Communication between teacher and students takes place in real time. A variety of technologies can provide this type of communication. These include fiber-optic lines (thin glass rods that transmit laser light impulses and are laid underground), microwave technology (where data are transmitted by a series of towers established across the terrain), and satellite.

Historically, two-way video/two-way audio has been stymied by the high cost of the broad bandwidth needed to transmit full-motion video. Past attempts to compress video resulted in poor-quality images. However, video compression techniques have improved dramatically. Video signals, when transmitted through fiber-optic lines, show virtually no loss of image quality (West 1991b). Currently, video images transmitted via microwave are not compressed. The compression of video images for delivery via satellite still presents some problems (e.g., "jerkiness" in the picture). However, a great deal of development work is being done in this area, and improvements and breakthroughs are measured by months rather than years.

At present, these systems are expensive by school standards. For example, the codecs (encoders/decoders) to convert (at the sender's site) the sender's analog signals to digital signals and (at the receiver's site) the digital signals back to analog currently cost about $20,000 to $30,000. Cameras and monitors, too, are expensive. There is a strong interest in making this technology more affordable, however. The Communications Competitiveness and Infrastructure Modernization Act, originally sponsored by Senators Al Gore and Conrad Burns, would set as a national goal the establishment of an "advanced, interactive. . .broad band communications system" to serve homes, schools, and other users, and to provide a "broad range of new educational opportunities for students of all ages." Many states are also investing a considerable amount of money in planning and establishing networks capable of providing two-way video/two-way audio. In Oregon, for example, Network 2 of the state's EdNet has been used by higher education institutions and became available to K-12 users in the fall of 1992.

One-Way Video/Two-Way Audio—Satellite technology can deliver relatively affordable instruction. Direct broadcast satellite (DBS) technology consists of high-powered satellite transmissions received by small, low-power receivers. These receivers are low in cost ($300 to $400) and easy to operate and install, making them good choices for the needs of individual schools (Douglas & Bransford 1991). In an attempt to reduce the costs of satellite communication (and thereby increase utilization), the EDSAT Institute, a not-for-profit organization, is actively working to bring to fruition a satellite dedicated to education (West 1991).

Audio/video signals can be broadcast via satellite to an unlimited number of sites and over large geographic areas. It should be noted, however, that limits must be placed on the number of receive sites to enable the teacher to handle effectively the load of students in multiple classrooms. The Los Angeles County School District recently launched a satellite education project beaming mathematics and science lessons (in English and in Spanish) to at-risk students. In this program, classroom teachers team up with the on-camera teachers in a new kind of team-teaching approach ("Technology-aided teaching," 1991).

When coupled with a telephone, satellite systems can provide live, one-way, full-motion video with two-way audio interactivity. This hybridizing of discrete technologies is a significant development in communication and can provide economical, customized systems to meet the needs of individuals, classrooms, schools, and districts (Douglas & Bransford 1991). Live-broadcast teachers can communicate in real time with the students in their audience, fine-tuning their instruction to meet student needs. Students may regard these one-way video/two-way audio, satellite-based systems as being similar to television; accordingly, production values must be high, and the teacher must be able to "perform" during the broadcast.

Other, newer hybrid systems are exemplified by the network emanating from Spokane, Washington's Educational School District (ESD) 101. This satellite-based network uses one video channel, one audio channel, and one data channel. The teacher interacts with students through the audio channel as he/she delivers instruction through video. At the same time, information (text and graphics) can be delivered from the teacher's site to the students' site, where it is captured on a computer. Students also use the channel to respond to the teacher after class hours, deliver homework assignments, and so on. A scanner is available at each school site, so students can input text and other data.

Telephone and Voicemail—Telephone companies are exploring a variety of educationally relevant services that they may begin offering over regular telephone lines. These include linking school or home computers to database services, voicemail services to keep parents informed of homework assignments and school activities, cellular telephones, and audiographic communication, including today's slow-scan visual images and future, faster imaging (Douglas & Bransford 1991).

Star Schools Program—The Star Schools program provides U.S. Department of Education funds for telecommunications projects offering instruction to students and training for teachers ("Educators Ask Not for the Moon," 1991). Star Schools programs bring together colleges, universities, and businesses to help schools acquire equipment (usually satellite or microwave, but also computers, modems, monitors, etc.) and instructional programming to improve science, mathematics, foreign language, and other subject instruction especially for students in Chapter 1 schools or students who lack access to instruction in those fields (FCCSET Committee on Education and Human Resources 1991). In 1988, the first year of the program, four demonstration projects were funded: three of the projects used video satellite broadcasts in conjunction with telephones and modems to achieve one-way video/two-way audio communication; one program used an electronic mail (e-mail) system. Four additional projects were funded in 1990. The Department of Education estimates that 6,000 schools are now participating with over 20,000 elementary and 20,000 high school students enrolled in Star Schools courses. New courses are being offered in advanced placement as well as those emphasizing higher-order thinking skills (Sheekey & Douglas 1991).

State and Regional Distance Learning Initiatives—The past decade has brought a dramatic increase in distance-learning in K-12 education, reflecting the rapid development of cost-effective, powerful communications technologies (Office of Technology Assessment 1989). Given the nature of the technology, systems are usually developed at the state or regional, rather than the local, level. Virtually all states are interested in using distance-learning technologies for K-12 education (Office of Technology Assessment 1989). States vary in the level at which they are currently implementing distance education projects: some have projects in place while others are in planning stages; some have postsecondary programs only but are looking to expand into elementary/secondary education (Office of Technology Assessment 1989).

Most state distance-learning projects involve hybrid systems (e.g., some combination of satellite, cable, computer network, and fiber-optic technologies). Many states are very active in distance-learning, including Alaska, Texas, Utah, Kansas, Kentucky, Washington, Oregon, and Iowa.

The Alaskan Teleconferencing Network and the University of Alaska Computer Network are used by school districts not only for electronic mail and teleconferencing, but also for the delivery of some instructional resources

(Office of Technology Assessment 1989). Video programming is used extensively in Alaska, where, often in small villages in isolated communities, many of the students fall into at-risk categories of one type or another. Video can be used to reduce the mental distance between communities there, provide more global views of the world, and increase students' motivation and involvement in education (Agency for Instructional Technology 1987).

The Texas Education Network (TENET), started in 1991, provides electronic mail, bulletin board, conferencing, and database capabilities to more than 4,300 public school users statewide. A commercial program started in Texas, TI-IN, provides live instructional broadcasts to more than 700 sites in 32 states.

Utah has a microwave communication system, EDNET, which is used for two-way audio and video presentation of high school instruction around the state. Other projects in Utah include using audiographic communications to deliver advanced placement courses and a distance-learning project using two-way cable/microwave technologies to link an elementary, a junior, and two senior high schools with the College of Eastern Utah (Office of Technology Assessment 1989).

Southwestern Bell Telephone Company is installing 168 miles of fiber optic cable for an interactive video network that will enable schools throughout Kansas to share teachers, with students at remote sites participating in class discussions via two-way video (Sheekey & Douglas 1991).

Kentucky is developing a statewide instructional satellite network, transmitting centrally to downlinks for each of the state's 1,300 elementary and secondary schools. Kentucky's plan calls for programming to be live and interactive (Office of Technology Assessment 1989).

Washington has a variety of distance-learning systems in place, including the one emanating from Spokane described above and the Washington Higher Education Telecommunications System (WHETS). WHETS is a microwave-based, two-way video/two-way audio system that connects multiple campuses.

In Oregon, EdNet provides one-way video, two-way audio capability to more than 100 schools and school districts and has also established a two-way video/two-way audio system network currently used by 40 institutions of higher education, state government agencies, and industry.

In Iowa a one-way video/two-way audio network has been initiated and is in the process of deployment.

Summary

The cooperative network projects described above illustrate how distance-learning can give students and teachers access to a broader range of resources and support collaborative projects involving complex themes. Collection and sharing of acid-rain data over the Kids Network or interaction with complex data sets and with astronauts and scientists over NASA's SpaceLink illustrate the interesting issues and access to experts that can be supported with a network. Involvement in such projects brings students into the realm of "real science" and involves them in more complex, abstract tasks

Table II-2

FEATURES OF EDUCATION REFORM AND SUPPORTIVE TECHNOLOGIES

Features of Education Reform							Potentially Supportive Technology
Heterogeneous Groupings	Performance-Based Assessment	Authentic and Multidisciplinary Tasks	Collaborative Work	Interactive Modes of Instruction	Student Exploration	Teacher as Facilitator	*Given a supportive instructional setting, the following technologies can support various features of reform, as indicated in this chart. It is possible to use the technologies in ways that promote other aspects of reform and many other exemplary products are currently available, but only uses and applications cited in the text are listed here.*
	●	●			●	●	**Electronic Databases** General discussion (pp. 19-20)
		●			●		**Electronic Reference Tools** Data Discman (p. 19) Encyclopedia Britannica (p. 19) The World Almanac and Book of Facts (p. 19)
●	●	●	●	●	●	●	**Hypermedia** Computer Supported Intentional Learning Environments (p. 26) Discover Rochester (p. 27) HyperCard (pp. 26-27)
				●		●	**Intelligent Computer-Assisted Instruction (ICAI)** General discussion (p. 15) Geometry Tutor (p. 15)
				●	●	●	**Intelligent Tools** Geometric Supposer (pp. 51-52)
		●	●		●	●	**Microcomputer-Based Labs** General discussion (pp. 15-20, 52-53)
	●	●	●	●	●	●	**Microworlds and Simulations** LOGO (pp. 20-21) LOGOWriter (p. 21) LegoLOGO (p. 21) Catlab (pp. 58, 67) Immigrant 1850 (pp. 44-45, 60-61) Palenque (p. 23) SimCity (p. 21) SimEarth (p. 21) Voyage of Mimi (pp. 17, 44) Where in the World is Carmen Sandiego? (pp. 21, 87)

Table II-2 (concluded)

Features of Education Reform							Potentially Supportive Technology
Heterogeneous Groupings	Performance-Based Assessment	Authentic and Multidisciplinary Tasks	Collaborative Work	Interactive Modes of Instruction	Student Exploration	Teacher as Facilitator	*Given a supportive instructional setting, the following technologies can support various features of reform, as indicated in this chart. It is possible to use the technologies in ways that promote other aspects of reform and many other exemplary products are currently available, but only uses and applications cited in the text are listed here.*
•	•	•	•		•	•	**Multimedia Tools and Approaches** Multimedia Works (pp. 27-28) Point of View (pp. 47, 53)
•	•	•	•	•	•	•	**Networks and Related Applications** Discourse System (p. 60) Earth Lab (pp. 50-51, 70, 83) FrEdMail (p. 29) Kids Network (pp. 29, 34, 49-50) Learning Circles (pp. 30, 48-49, 63-65) Learning Network (pp. 30, 48, 63-65) Network 2 (p. 32) SpaceLink (pp. 30, 34)
•				•		•	**Two-way Video/Two-way Audio Distance Learning** General discussion (pp. 29, 31-37) EDNET (pp. 32, 34) TENET (p. 34) WHETS (p. 34)
•	•	•	•		•	•	**Videocameras, VCRs, Editors** MicroMacro Lab (p. 60) VideoPals (p. 31)
		•	•	•	•	•	**Videodisc and CD-ROM** The Adventures of Jasper Woodbury (pp. 22-23) Animal Pathfinders (p. 23) Civil War Interactive (p. 23) The War in the Persian Gulf (p. 47) GTV (pp. 23, 86)
	•	•	•		•	•	**Word Processors/Intelligent Writing Tools** General Discussion (pp. 25-26) Writing Partner (p. 79) TextBrowser (pp. 61-62, 69)

than they generally encounter within individual classrooms. Outside scientific domains, the prospects of "publishing" and sending work to other students at a distance provide authenticity and importance to tasks that are often viewed as mundane when undertaken for the benefit of a classroom teacher.

Two-way video/two-way audio and one-way video/two-way audio are providing larger groups of students with access to instruction in advanced courses and to exemplary teachers. If used merely to present lectures to groups of students, however, these technologies do not fulfill their potential to support active student-centered learning. States have exerted leadership in developing the infrastructure for interactive distance-learning. What we need now are models for effective instruction using the full capabilities of the technology in ways that support collaborative learning with complex, authentic tasks. Just as it took some time for educators to develop effective ways to use computer networks (e.g., early efforts to set up one-on-one computerpals were less effective than subsequent group projects with a content focus; see Riel & Levin 1990), it will probably be some time before the best practices with interactive video technologies are discovered and disseminated.

Relating Technologies to Education Reform

The above review is intended as an overview of the range of instructional technologies found in schools and the ways in which those technologies can be used. Returning to our central concern with education reform, Table II-2 relates these technologies (and the specific applications used as examples) to the features of education reform discussed in Chapter I. The chart is intended for use as a guide directing the reader to technologies and applications discussed in this report that exemplify the supporting role that instructional technology can play in education reform. It should be noted that almost any of the technologies can support additional aspects of reform and that there are many more applications available that support reform-oriented instruction. This chapter and Table II-2 are intended as examples of the kinds of support that technologies can provide rather than as an exhaustive catalogue.

Availability of Instructional Technologies

The past decade has brought an explosive growth in both the number and the variety of applications of computers and other technologies used in schools. Although much of the available survey data has focused on the numbers and percentages of various technologies in the schools, some data are available on the ways in which technologies (especially computers) are used. Reviewed below are pertinent data on the availability of computers, modems and networks, VCRs and educational videos, CD-ROM and videodisc technologies, and satellite telecommunications links.

The Johns Hopkins University's Center for Social Organization of Schools has conducted three extensive surveys of U.S. school computer use over the last decade: in 1983 (see Becker 1985), in 1985 (see Becker & Sterling 1987), and, as part of the 1989 International Association for the Evaluation of

Educational Achievement (IEA) Computers in Education Survey, in the spring of 1989 (see Becker 1990). Other survey information has been reported by two marketing research firms that specialize in educational technology: Quality Education Data, Inc., (QED) and Market Data Retrieval, Inc.

Computers

Numbers of Computers—Becker (1990) chronicled the rapid growth of computers in public schools from fewer than 50,000 in 1983 to approximately 2.6 million in 1990. More recent estimates (Mageau 1991a) place the number of computers installed in U.S. schools (public and nonpublic) at 3.5 million. In percentage terms, in 1981 only about 18 percent of U.S. public schools had one or more computers for instruction; by 1987 that percentage had grown to 95 percent (Office of Technology Assessment 1988) and in 1990 it reached 97 percent (Becker 1990). Current estimates put the percentage of public schools with at least one computer at 98 percent (Mageau 1991a). In other words, nearly every school has at least one computer. The more pertinent question becomes the number of computers per school and per student.

The median number of computers in computer-using K-6 elementary schools rose from about 3 in 1985 to about 18 in 1989. In high schools the median number of computers rose from about 16 in 1985 to about 39 in 1989 (Becker 1990). The average number of computers per 30 students nearly tripled between 1984 and 1990, rising from 0.60 to 1.53 (Mageau 1991a). Although the numbers of computers per school and per student have increased dramatically from the mid-1980s to the early 1990s, student access to computers must still be considered limited. In 1987, students averaged only 1 hour each week on a computer (Office of Technology Assessment 1988). Even the recent computer:student ratio of 1.53:30 conjures up images of classes of students jockeying for time on a limited number of machines. The most common arrangement is a computer lab of 20 to 30 machines into which whole classes are scheduled for small amounts of time. Most schools do not have enough computers for them to be used frequently by all or most students.

How Computers Are Being Used—In 1983, computers were used primarily for three tasks: to teach students about computers (i.e., computer literacy classes), to teach programming, and for rote learning through drill-and-practice programs (Becker 1985). In 1985, teachers reported using computers primarily for enrichment and variety, or for teaching students about computers, and rarely to provide students with instruction in core academic subjects (Becker 1990). This reported pattern of use supports the argument that technology is used at the margins but not as an integral part of schooling.

A more recent trend noted by Becker (1990) is increasing use of computers as tools and less emphasis on teaching about computers per se than in 1985. At the same time, use of computers to teach basic skills continues to be the dominant practice in elementary schools and is increasing in high schools.

Integrated learning systems (ILSs) represent an increasingly common application of computers to basic skills instruction. Approximately 10,000 ILSs are currently in use, funded primarily with Chapter 1 monies (Mageau 1990).

QED survey results (cited in Becker 1990) indicate that, as of 1990 1.4 percent of public schools had integrated learning systems. ILSs, then, represent a small niche in the educational applications of computers, but given their funding from programs for disadvantaged students, they represent a significant use of technology for this group.

Modems and Networks

Networks are systems that connect two or more computers to each other. These computers can be at distant sites, allowing students or teachers to communicate with peers or with each other districtwide, statewide, nationally, or even internationally. Networks can also be local. Locally networked computers have numerous advantages (Becker 1990): they do not require software programs on multiple copies of floppy disks; they give students access to databases; they allow several computers to share a single printer; and they promote collaborative writing. In spite of these advantages, only 24 percent of high schools and only 7 percent of elementary schools had networked computers in 1989 (Becker 1990). Networks represent an area ripe for rapid growth.

Modems allow for communication between computers at remote sites. In the 1988-1989 school year, approximately 25 percent of schools had modems; during the 1991-1992 school year, this percentage was expected to double to 50 percent (Mageau 1991a). Modems can be used to connect schools to network services, such as Prodigy or CompuServe, or to access other institutions participating in a wide area network (WAN). Many teachers use Internet, a system developed by the National Science Foundation to connect universities, government, and research centers.

Newman (1992b) notes that most local area networks (LANs) within schools are used to deliver tutorial instruction as part of an integrated learning system. In 1990 only a small minority of schools had both LANs and access to wide area networks. Even when they did, the computers on the LAN were seldom connected to the WAN, and hence the networks were not being used to provide large numbers of students with data and communication from the outside world. Despite lots of talk about telecommunications tearing down the school walls, neither the basic technology infrastructure nor the understanding of how best to capitalize on it is common at present. The potential is there, however. Plans are being developed for a National Research and Education Network (NREN), which would connect schools to major research and information centers, providing students and their teachers with access to information, databases, and special instruments, such as supercomputers, telescopes, or particle accelerators (Hunter 1992).

VCRs and Educational Video

Chen (1991) has noted that the best national data on instructional television use are the 7-year-old estimates from the School Utilization Study funded by the Corporation for Public Broadcasting. According to this study, 54 percent of the nation's teachers used instructional television, one-third of them using at least two television series.

QED data indicate that between 1982 and 1989 the number of schools using videotapes more than tripled, from 31 percent to 99 percent—near total saturation (Chen 1991). During these same years, the number of VCRs increased threefold from 26,000 to 81,000 (Chen 1991). Reports indicate that 91 percent to 96 percent of schools own at least one VCR (Becker 1990; Mageau 1991a). VCRs have taken their place in schools as a basic technology for education.

CD-ROM and Videodiscs

A recent QED survey found that, of approximately 15,000 school districts in the United States, 1,377 had CD-ROM drives, representing an increase of 70 percent over the previous year (Yoder 1991). Videodisc players were in use in 1,273 districts, a figure up 38 percent from the previous year (Yoder 1991). CD-ROM players, then, were in use in about 9 percent of the school districts and videodisc players in about 8.5 percent of the districts. QED predicted that both CD-ROM and videodisc use in schools would more than double during the 1991-1992 school year. Thus, although CD-ROM and videodisc technologies are available in only a small percentage of schools and school districts currently, with expected decreases in cost, they will become increasingly common.

Satellite Technologies

Distance-learning programs are currently supported in nearly every state. Many of these programs focus on using satellite technologies to instruct children in isolated communities. An estimated one-third of all rural schools have telecommunications links; about one-third of these receive funding through the U.S. Department of Education's Star Schools program. Data suggest that 15 percent to 16 percent of public schools have satellite dishes (Becker 1990; Mageau 1991a).

Projections for the Future

After 1981, the number of public schools with computers increased around 11 percent annually (Office of Technology Assessment 1988). Approximately 300,000 to 400,000 computers have been added each year to U.S. schools (Becker 1990). Given the current number of computers in U.S. schools (about 2.6 million), if the number of computers added annually remains constant, we can anticipate about 4.2 million computers in public schools by 1995 and 6 million by the turn of the century. This projection is only slightly more conservative than the projection of 4.8 million computers in 1994 for public and private schools combined offered by LINK Resources (Mageau 1991a). If current trends continue, the median number of computers per school will rise from today's 33 to about 51 in 1995 and 74 in the year 2000. These average figures will mask large differences among schools, however, with some schools, districts, and states providing near universal access to computers, while others offer very little.

Equity Issues

Even with an anticipated major increase in computers and other technologies overall, there is concern that subgroups of students may have unequal access to these resources. Schools serving high socioeconomic status students report higher computer-to-student ratios than do schools with low socioeconomic status students (Becker 1983; Becker & Sterling 1987). The National Assessment of Educational Progress (NAEP) 1985-1986 survey found that white students were more likely to have used a computer than were African-American or Hispanic students, although this difference diminished at the high school level (Sutton 1991).

The problem is exacerbated by large differences in access to computers in the home. The NAEP survey found that nearly one-third of white high school students owned computers, compared with a little over one-fifth of African-American and Hispanic students (Sutton 1991). In 1985, African-American students were less likely to attend elementary schools with computers and, at both the elementary and secondary levels, tended to attend schools with fewer computer-using teachers than did white students (Becker & Sterling 1987). Higher socioeconomic status and white students, then, are more likely to have access to computers for education than are lower socioeconomic status and minority students.

Although smaller than socioeconomic and ethnicity differences, there is also a gender difference in access to computers in the schools, with boys having more access than girls (Sutton 1991). In addition, families of male students are more likely to own computers than are families of female students, and boys are more likely than girls to attend summer computer camps (Sutton 1991). Finally, academically more able students tend to use computers more than less able students (Becker & Sterling 1987).

Even when access to computers is equivalent, there may be important differences among groups in the way computers are used. Students in low-ability classes tend to use computers for drill and practice, while higher-ability students tend to use them more broadly, in ways that are more congruent with education reform goals (Becker & Sterling 1987; DeVillar & Faltis 1991).

In summary, research indicates that higher socioeconomic status students, white students, male students, and higher-ability students tend to use computers more than lower socioeconomic status students, minority students, female students, and lower-ability students. Comparable data are not available on other technologies, but similar patterns are likely to be common to many of them. If we consider access to the kind of collaborative, student-centered learning of advanced skills we have described above, inequalities are almost certainly even greater. Convincing those who develop instructional programs for disadvantaged students and those who purchase equipment and software with Chapter 1 funds of the appropriateness of challenging, technology-based projects for their students is one step in confronting the inequality. Even so, policymakers will need to address the issue of the proper state and federal roles in addressing the fundamental problem of large differences in the funds available for technology purchase and implementation.

Chapter III
Support for Student Learning Activities

Capabilities Provided by Technology

Technology offers powerful support for learning skills through inquiry and problem solving. In this chapter, we explore specific ways in which technology enables the kind of challenging instruction depicted in the right-hand portion of Figure I-1. Technology can promote student exploration through collaborative involvement in authentic, challenging multidisciplinary tasks by providing realistic complex environments for student inquiry, furnishing information and tools to support investigation, linking classrooms for joint investigations, and presenting data in ways that support mathematical thinking and problem-solving.

Realistic Complex Environments for Inquiry

Teachers can draw on technology applications to simulate real-world environments and create actual environments for experimentation, so that students can carry out authentic tasks as real workers would, explore new terrains, meet people of different cultures, and use a variety of tools to gather information and solve problems. Working on "authentic tasks," which Brown, Collins, and Duguid (1989) define simply as the ordinary practices of the culture, engages students in sustained exploration and provides multiple opportunities to reflect on the decisions made in trying to address the problem. Authentic tasks are highly motivating for students, leading them to acquire advanced skills and knowledge because they become engrossed in the problems that, for example, navigators, anthropologists, or historians face. Just as important, simulations address the problem of "inert knowledge." Many typical school tasks are stripped of the meanings and the context that they hold for real practitioners. In learning tasks in this stripped-down form, students are unable to extract anything that they can apply in richer, more complex situations outside of school (The Cognition and Technology Group at Vanderbilt 1990; Sherwood, Kinzer, Bransford, and Franks 1987; Whitehead 1929). "Case-based instruction," as it was termed by earlier writers (Gragg 1940), presents students with the same problems that expert practitioners attempt and provides a motivating environment for cooperative learning and teacher-directed mediation (Bransford, Goin, Hasselbring, Kinzer, Sherwood & Williams 1988; Bransford, Sherwood, Hasselbring, Kinzer & Williams 1989). Simulated environments allow students to get involved with the problem, often through visual media, which provide integrated context and help students comprehend new ideas more easily (Hasselbring, Goin, Zhou, Alcantara & Musil 1992).

Simulations are student centered, since students make decisions and see the results of their actions. The teacher is present, but in the role of coach, using discussion to prompt students to explore different aspects of the problem space, answering students' questions, and encouraging students to elaborate their thinking and listen to other points of view. Because the problem space is always accessible (unlike real-life situations), students can revisit and revise their conceptual understanding. The nature of the teacher–student relationship is altered as both become co-learners; knowledge is constructed in collaboration rather than transmitted from teacher to student. Students help each other learn, working together in a generative and cooperative environment (Center for Technology in Education 1991). The examples below are provided as illustrations of how technology can support student involvement in authentic tasks.

Voyage of the Mimi—Since 1985, when it first became available for commercial use, teachers have been using *The Voyage of the Mimi I,* developed by Bank Street College, to create environments for exploration. The centerpiece of the first voyage is a 13-part television drama that portrays the adventures of a group of young scientists, including several adolescents, who are studying whales off the coast of New England. Viewers observe the crew conducting scientific experiments and solving technical problems. A separate documentary accompanies each television show, portraying scientists engaged in their work. Four computer modules engage students in using navigation concepts and instruments, for example, to free a trapped whale in the Atlantic. The modules also include a microworld ecosystem, a tool for measuring and graphing physical events, and a programming environment. A book version of the TV show, classroom activities, and additional resources are also available for teachers.

Not all of the *Voyage of the Mimi* environments are simulated. One video shows young scientists studying the sound frequencies of whales. In their classroom labs, students can then carry out careful studies of their own voices and of musical instruments and create real-time audio frequency spectra.

The Second Voyage of the Mimi exposes students to archaeology and to the culture of the ancient Maya in Mexico's Yucatan peninsula. The goal of the curriculum is "to motivate children's interest in science as a 'real-world' activity, and to make various scientific concepts understandable to a wide range of children" (Wilson 1987, p. 1). The multimedia package includes a 12-episode television series as well as two software programs—*Maya Math* and *Sun Lab*.

The latest development effort by the Bank Street researchers/developers of the Mimi materials is the Palenque project, a digital video interactive (DVI) prototype described in Chapter II. The locations and several of the characters from *The Second Voyage of the Mimi* have been used again in the Palenque project. Palenque embodies the same instructional strategy as its Mimi predecessors in a DVI system that provides for electronic as well as thematic integration (Wilson & Tally 1991).

Immigrant 1850—Developed by Project Zero at Harvard University, *Immigrant 1850* encourages students (upper elementary through high school) to identify with the Irish immigrant experience of the mid 1800s by taking on the role of one who leaves Ireland to face the difficulties of establishing a new life in Boston (Morrison & Walters 1989; Walters & Gardner 1990; Walters & Gardner 1991). Students have access to a core set of computer-based activities in which they can adopt an immigrant family and "live through" the complex decisions the family may have made in finding housing and a job, calculating finances, and shopping within their earnings. Students can use a database, spreadsheet, and word processor to calculate expenses and keep diaries. In multiple rounds of field testing *Immigrant 1850* with more than 100 classrooms, researchers found that both regular and special-needs students could sustain involvement with this learning environment for periods ranging from several weeks to an entire school year.

Many teachers involved with the *Immigrant 1850* unit used the existing materials as a starting point to create additional innovative learning environments for their particular students, drawing on additional technology applications (e.g., an extensive on-line, visual database) and corollary activities (e.g., tracking the population of American cities, Indian tribes in Texas, etc.). Researchers also found that some teachers used *Immigrant 1850* as a model to create their own engaging computer-based curriculum units (Walters & Gardner 1991).

In all of these programs, the technology both draws groups of students into a richly complex setting—a whaling vessel, muddy streets of an earlier Boston, a Mayan city—that stimulates their questions and provides them with the resources to gather and integrate information themselves. Thus, these technology applications support student exploration, engagement with complex, multidisciplinary tasks, and collaborative work. The benefits of these authentic, challenging environments for students increase as both teachers and students get comfortable with the materials and the various learning pathways within them.

Information and Tools to Support Investigation

The applications just described provide the content, the materials, and the varied pathways students can follow in learning through interaction with a simulation. Alternatively, technology can be used to enable students to investigate questions within curriculum units that individual teachers or teams of teachers have designed. Teachers make accessible to students technology applications that allow students to gather information (e.g., CD-ROM, videodiscs); to store, organize, and analyze information (databases, spreadsheets, timelines, graphing programs); and to represent and convey to others what they have learned (multimedia applications, desktop publishing, graphics programs). As discussed in Chapter II, these technologies are primarily general-purpose tools. The essence of the innovation lies in the development of an instructional framework within which these tools are used. The overarching themes and "big questions" investigated in these projects are usually interdisciplinary, and they need to be carefully selected to respond to students' developmental needs and interests and to reflect issues of social and scientific consequence. Students work individually or in collaboration with others in these inquiry-oriented units, and work over extended periods of time on projects culminating in presentations or "exhibitions" that provide the basis for assessing their learning.

Two examples of projects using technology to provide information and tools for student inquiry are provided below.

MAKE IT HAPPEN!—In four middle schools in New York, Massachusetts, and New Hampshire, teachers used a rich variety of technology applications within an interdisciplinary, I-Search unit (based on the work of Macrorie 1988). An I-Search unit has four instructional phases:

- Phase 1: Teachers immerse students in a theme or topic, eliciting students' prior knowledge, helping students build background knowledge, and motivating students to choose a personally meaningful question to explore.

- Phase 2: Students develop a search plan for gathering information and building knowledge.

- Phase 3: Students gather and integrate information.

- Phase 4: Students develop an I-Search Report and disseminate to others what they have learned.

The teachers implementing this approach were field testing *MAKE IT HAPPEN!*, a manual developed by Education Development Center based on 5 years of research and development (Zorfass et al. 1989; 1991; Zorfass, Morocco & Lory 1991). *MAKE IT HAPPEN!* guides interdisciplinary teams of teachers in designing and implementing an I-Search Unit. Each of the four field test sites carried out a different inquiry-based, thematic unit that integrated various technology applications.

In a suburb of New York City, the unit was on the human body. Teachers and students used simulations (*The Human Body Pump*, *Inner Body Works*, *Life and Death*), a CD-ROM magazine index, videos, and word processing. The suburban Boston school in this study implemented a unit focused on Africa ("Dispelling the Myth of the Dark Continent") . Teachers and students used videos, word processing, *MacPaint*, and *Inspiration* (a mind-mapping and outlining tool). In a rural community in New Hampshire, the unit focused on the history of the town. The technology that became part of the unit included *TimeLiner*, *meccGraph*, a teacher-made video, a database program, and word processing. In a small urban area in Massachusetts, the unit was on "Race and Culture." Besides using videos and filmstrips, the students used *The New Grolier Electronic Encyclopedia* and word processing.

Across all four schools, every student identified a question that he or she felt motivated to investigate. Students commented that they felt like explorers, learned information that would affect their lives, and found new ways of gathering, organizing, and conveying information:

I-Search has been a good opportunity for me. I liked leaving the classroom and going into the community to do my research. I met and interviewed important people. They were experts. At the museum I had the chance to "try it myself," not just read about it in books. These things showed me how fast I could learn just by asking questions and trying it. And I was happy when everyone was so willing to help me. (Student from New Hampshire)

This research taught me how to do a report an easier and more creative way. Books aren't your only source. You could interview people or go to a place that might have information. This means to me that I didn't have to use all books. I went and talked to someone about their life and was surprised that she would share something like that with me. (Student from New Hampshire)

Software Evaluation Project—Middle school social studies students participating in the Software Evaluation Project at the State University of New York at Buffalo used technology to navigate their own paths through a vast body of data (P. Stearns 1991b). By using a series of multimedia resources, including *Point of View, The New Grolier Electronic Encyclopedia,* and the CD-ROM interactive videodisc *The War in the Persian Gulf,* teachers created a research environment that both motivated and guided the students in searching for and presenting information. Within the classwide theme of the Persian Gulf War, small teams of students worked cooperatively to research particular aspects of the war that interested them and then created a culminating multimedia presentation. Using the software program *Point of View* as an authoring tool for the presentation, students were able to articulate their insights about complex issues (P. Stearns 1991a; 1991b).

Students take the initiating role in these classroom-designed curriculum units, with the teachers in a support and facilitating role. Rather than transmitting a body of facts and information about the subject to the students, teachers used technology applications such as *Point of View* to stimulate and then help structure the students' individual or small-group investigations. One teacher introduced that program using a projection system, then asked students to suggest various paths for exploration of the different lists. Even during the class demonstration, students could take the initiative to move around in the system, looking at maps, charts, documents, and text, and suggesting keywords for searching for information. Once students were working on individual or small-group projects, the teacher provided guidance when students needed it as they searched for information and pictures and wrote brief essays to include in their presentations. Encouraged to carry out their investigations with partners, students got help from teachers when they needed it to work effectively in cooperative small groups.

Peggy Healy Stearns (in press), like others researching computer-supported inquiry programs, finds that students sustain a high level of interest and curiosity when they are using a database to explore their own questions. According to Stearns, "The information that students retrieved in their investigations took on special significance because the questions were their own and the answers were viewed as personal discoveries. Students had a sense of ownership that is absent when they are spoon fed".

Programs such as *MAKE IT HAPPEN!,* the Software Evaluation project, and the Discover Rochester program described in Chapter II use technology extensively, but they are critically dependent on the teacher to set the context, model appropriate research strategies, and, until students become more expert computer users, cue students to the ways that technology can help them over the course of their projects. It is the selection of complex, interdisciplinary topics to explore, organization of learning into long-term inquiry-based units, and setting up of collaborative work teams that constitute the heart of the innovation. Technology supports this kind of work and adds to students' sense of excitement and belief that they are doing something important. An additional benefit of technology is that the resulting projects are motivating because they look much more professional than conventional student work. In addition, the projects provide a stronger basis for meaningful assessment.

Link Classrooms for Joint Investigations

Computer networks enable students and teachers to move the learning process beyond the boundaries of the classroom and into the world outside school (Newman 1992a). By bringing telecommunications applications into their classrooms, teachers create environments where students can communicate via electronic mail with other students, participate in collaborative projects, and gather and pool information in a joint endeavor to understand issues.

Learning Circles—The AT&T Learning Network links classes from geographically diverse locations into "learning circles" to accomplish shared educational goals (Riel 1991a). The network matches teachers and their students with seven to nine other classrooms that share academic interests but represent different geographic or cultural perspectives. As noted in Chapter II, each classroom within a learning circle has the opportunity to design projects and request information from the other circle partners for these projects. Examples of student-conducted research projects include how weather and seasonal patterns affect the daily lives of people in different locations, the influence of mass media on children's lives, and a survey of cities in transition (Riel 1990a; 1990b). Students in New York, Australia, and Canada, as well as other distant locations, researched and then traded stories about the history of their own communities. After collecting the information from their distant partners via the telecommunications network, the students worked with the information they received—analyzing, evaluating, synthesizing, and eventually publishing the project in a cooperative learning circle publication.

A learning circle network fosters authentic inquiry-based learning by providing real purpose, motivation, and audience for students to conduct research and write to one another. Students are not working on arbitrary assignments but on novel tasks that were designed by their learning circle partners.

The telecommunications environment provides students with opportunities to develop new awareness and appreciation of individual differences that teachers could not provide within the boundaries of their own classrooms. Research suggests that students are better able to function as an intellectual critic for distant peers than for themselves or classmates and that they learn to write better when physical distance makes clear the need to provide explicit content for the reader (Riel 1992). An additional advantage is that physical and sensory limitations become "invisible" in this medium, since the recipients of messages in one classroom do not know what special efforts the senders may have made in order to communicate. In one learning circle, a classroom sent around an introductory packet about themselves to the other classes, including an audiotape of stories from the class. Another class in the circle was made up of hearing-impaired students who wrote back a cogent and personal statement about what it is like to be deaf and how they are often treated as stupid (Riel 1992).

Riel (1990b) finds that relationships between students and their teachers change in learning circle projects. The teacher becomes a learner alongside students as each classroom designs activities for the learning circle and participates in other circle partners' investigations. Unlike a typical self-contained lesson in which the classroom teacher plans and implements an activity, individual classroom teachers do not have total control over the direction of a learning circle project. They do not know what students and teachers in other locations will contribute to the process and cannot predict the exact course the project will take. Instead, the students see the teachers in the role of a participant in the learning process. In this role, the teacher serves as a model of active learning—setting a powerful example for students.

TERC Network Science Programs—Over the past decade, Technical Educational Research Centers (TERC) has been linking groups of classrooms to each other and to professional scientists who can help students explore pressing global questions. TERC's network science programs are based on the premise that students can carry out scientific investigations with real scientists and that computers can enhance this enterprise (Julyan 1991). Students conduct experiments, analyze data, and share results with their colleagues using a simple computer-based telecommunications network. This collecting and making sense of data gives the students an opportunity "to experience the excitement of science that scientists feel" (Julyan 1991, p. 5).

Kids Network. One of the TERC network projects, the National Geographic Kids Network, involves students and teachers across the United States and in a number of foreign countries working collaboratively on science projects (TERC 1990). The project is funded by the National Science Foundation (NSF) and the National Geographic Society (NGS) and is now published by NGS. The initial unit of the Kids Network involved teachers and students in fourth through sixth grade from 200 schools in a study of acid rain.

Students collected data on the pH of their local water, then shared this data with the other schools on the telecommunications network. Using a word processor, data/record-keeping software, graphing utility, map software with data overlay, and telecommunications package (Julyan 1991), students were able to display their own data and the combined data from other schools in tables, graphs, and maps and then compare and analyze the data. The scientist who was involved in the project communicated with the students over the network, answering questions, commenting on their data, and suggesting ways they might analyze their data (Lenk 1988).

Since that initial unit, TERC has developed five other units for fourth-through sixth-grade students. Each unit involves students examining the topic in their local community and then guides them in expanding the inquiry by sharing data with other students in distant locations (Julyan 1991). The themes of the curriculum units are "Too Much Trash," "What's in Our Water?," "Weather in Action," "What are We Eating?," and "Solar Energy." Whenever possible, a professional scientist is involved in the unit, communicating with students over the network. Currently, TERC is developing nine Kids Network units for sixth- through ninth-grade classrooms, beginning with a unit on the human body.

TERC Star Schools. TERC developed another network project, the Star Schools project, involving secondary students and teachers from across the country and recognized resource centers. These groups collaborated to create a new learning environment in which students work together to tackle compelling problems, such as measuring radon levels in their schools, designing solar houses, collecting weather data, and exploring "mathematical chaos" (Berger 1989). Teachers feel that this environment allows students to realize that important problems are complex and may have more than one solution.

Earth Lab—The initial and primary goal of the Earth Lab project, directed by Denis Newman of Bolt, Beranek and Newman, Inc., was to create classroom environments in which students used collaborative workspaces to learn elementary earth science in much the same way as scientists do (Newman 1992a). All of the computers in the school were connected via a local area network (LAN) to a hard-disk drive, which allowed for central storage of data, text, and programs. A network interface such as this makes it very easy for individuals or groups to store and retrieve data that pertains to their projects. Students and teachers can be assigned to any number of independent or collaborative workspaces.

Although the most obvious effect of these computer-supported, global laboratories is that they open the boundaries of the classroom to global investigations, Newman's work shows that they are also affecting boundaries between classrooms and subject areas within the school. When teachers had access to the Earth Lab network, they created environments for teaching and learning that were decompartmentalized (Newman 1990a). Students in the network were more likely to carry their work from one context to another. They continued to work on assignments, both individually and cooperatively, even after class periods ended, on whatever computer they found available. Since their workspaces were always accessible from any computer, students had greater autonomy to choose when to continue work on their projects. As a result, the computer lab was increasingly used in a "heterogeneous manner" with groups of students from several classes working on different projects simultaneously.

Ironically, in opening up boundaries between the school and other parts of the globe, communication boundaries also appeared to shift between teachers and students in local schools. As part of the Earth Lab project, the electronic mail system was made available for both student and teacher use. Researchers found that students and teachers carried on individual conversations, something that rarely occurred in the regular classroom (Newman 1990a; 1992a).

Supporting Mathematical and Scientific Thinking

Computers, with their calculation, database, and graphic capabilities, support the work of practicing scientists and mathematicians. It is highly appropriate that they be used also to support student learning in these areas. Software specifically designed for this purpose is starting to gain acceptance in schools, as illustrated by the examples that follow.

Geometric Supposer—*Geometric Supposer* is a set of microcomputer software tools developed by Judah Schwartz and Michal Yerushalmy to teach high school geometry through a guided-inquiry approach. The Supposers allow the user to make geometric constructions of the sort created with a compass and straightedge. The software includes a facility to measure angles, areas, and line segments and to perform arithmetic operations on these numerical data. The software remembers a construction as a procedure and allows the user to repeat the construction on another geometric figure of the same sort (Wiske & Houde 1988). Students engage in inductive thinking and have a chance to "reinvent" definitions and theorems and to explore new and interesting and complex geometric ideas (Yerushalmy, Chazan & Gordon 1988).

In a year-long research project on the implementation of a guided inquiry approach using *Geometric Supposer* in three Boston area suburbs during the 1985-86 school year, project staff assessed student learning and examined implementation issues (Yerushalmy, Chazan & Gordon 1988). Interviews with a sample of "best" and "worst" students found that students had no technical difficulties with the software. However, nearly all students found the guided-inquiry approach more difficult than traditional, textbook mathematics and experienced some frustration. Many found conjecture-making difficult, and in general students voiced a need for direction and guidance. Some students became adept at stepping back to observe the teacher role and think about the kind of support that they needed. They did not want simplification of the problem or step-by-step procedures as much as a clearer sense of direction and close support as they began a challenge:

> [If I were teaching] when I started out, I would discuss it more; I'd show more of how to do things. Then as you got more and more into the thing, I'd ease off and let people figure it out for themselves.

The researchers found that in general students understood the power of the guided-inquiry approach and enjoyed learning that way, particularly when they were successful. They liked working with the computer, using the tools to make conjectures, and felt that they grasped the content more deeply as a result. At times, they had a real experience of discovery. Some students found themselves using conjectural thinking beyond the mathematics classroom:

> If somebody, a teacher or anybody, tells you something, you think maybe it could be this. You have a bunch of ideas. Not just two, but a bunch of them. You're thinking what could be the reason for it? You have a list of ideas going through your mind. Then you sit down and play it out or figure it out.

> I always make conjectures now about little things. I don't know. It's very hard to explain. I'll be in another class. You see how things work, so you make a conjecture and you generalize about other things. Especially in biology because it's life in general. It's so interesting. You can just make conjectures.

The research found that teachers using *Geometric Supposer* through a guided-inquiry approach need to "strike a productive balance between providing thoughtful guidance and freedom for students to investigate their own ideas, falling neither into intellectual tyranny nor into abdication of responsibility" (Wiske 1990, p. 8). Teachers need to be "active learners in the classroom, modeling the activities of wondering, conjecturing, being mistaken or stymied, and proceeding without knowing whether they were on the right track" (Wiske 1990, p. 8).

Microcomputer-Based Laboratories—As described in Chapter II, microcomputer-based laboratories (MBLs) are tools teachers can bring into the classroom to expand the range of students' learning in science. These tools can include a dozen sensors, a lab interface, and a low-cost microcomputer, allowing students to have measurement and computational power that can support projects where they do actual measurements. Tinker and Papert (1989) point out that MBL is a realization of an earlier dream of science educators: a flexible instrument that speeds up computations related to force, light, pressure, temperature, heart rate, speed, etc. Equally important, the instrument leaves students the choice about what computations to use (p. 9).

Although the MBL equipment can facilitate open-ended exploration, the laboratory lessons used by teachers typically direct students to gather and analyze specific data as they perform particular experiments (Wiske, Niguidula & Shepard 1988, p. 7). The MBL lessons are based on the belief that students today hold many of the misconceptions about heat and temperature once held by scientists. Simple instruction will not change deeply held misconceptions; rather, experiments need to stimulate students to fundamentally reorganize their understanding. This view echoes a constructionist perspective (Papert 1988) that students learn best through active engagement in their own studies in an environment that encourages them to construct and communicate their own knowledge and understandings. Consistent with this perspective, some of the experiments that helped earlier scientists begin to question their concepts of thermal physics are incorporated into these materials, so that students can actively examine and reconstruct their own understanding (Wiske, Niguidula & Shepard 1988).

Use of MBLs in schools with teachers and students indicates that real and accurate measurements motivate students, especially if student work mirrors scientific research. However, field testing has also revealed that teachers need to structure the environment to make learning efficient. Teachers have noted how important it is for students to communicate findings through class discussion, writing in lab guides, or informal student conversation in small groups.

Challenges for Students Using Technology

Many adults have feared that students, especially so-called "at-risk students," would become frustrated by the technical demands of the kinds of technologies described above. Experience suggests to the contrary that learning the technical aspects of working with technology is not a major problem for most students. Students face several other kinds of challenges when they use technology to support them in active, inquiry learning, however. These include:

- understanding their responsibilities as active learners;

- getting help with individual learning needs; and

- integrating their technology-supported inquiry learning with their larger school experience.

Understanding Their Responsibilities as Active Learners

Authentic inquiry tasks provide exciting new challenges for students and can also require a host of advanced intellectual and social learning skills, involving new levels of independence. Peggy Healy Stearns (1991c) noted that for many of the students participating in the Software Evaluation Project and using *Point of View* to create multimedia presentations, working in cooperative groups was an innovation in its own right. The social studies teacher needed to help students develop productive working relationships, so that they could cooperatively research the topics and create a presentation to share with their classmates.

Teachers in that project and others we have discussed find that they need to explain to students explicitly that their responsibilities in these programs are different from the usual role of "listening, remembering, and repeating what the teacher told them" (Wiske 1990, p. 8). Developing their own questions is the reverse of the role that many students have honed—anticipating answers to factual and narrowly focused teacher questions. Students' difficulties with conjecturing with *Geometric Supposer* were more acute when teachers did not provide clear models and facilitation, and students did not grasp the kind of thinking they were to do.

> You have to start it all on your own. She'll [the teacher] give us a
> little something. The sheets that we work on will say a little something.
> We have to come up with everything. That's what we're supposed to do.
> We're not complaining. It's just a little hard   sometimes. Maybe we are
> complaining.

> He lets us do anything we want for conjectures, but it doesn't help me at
> all in thinking them up.

More important, the kinds of inquiry learning teachers are trying to catalyze with *Voyage of the Mimi, Geometric Supposer*, and technology-supported inquiry learning in the *MAKE IT HAPPEN!* program may challenge students' fundamental view of what teaching and learning are all about. With these innovations, learning is no longer a process in which a teacher who knows all passes on knowledge and students passively take it in. Grasping how different her work with *Geometric Supposer* was from her other classes, one student mused that:

> It's different. It's like abstract thinking. It's different than anything
> else you've ever done—maybe a little harder than I expected. We have
> to think about everything that you learn, instead of just having a
> teacher teach you, memorize it, and just do it. You have to think about
> it yourself. (Yerushalmy, Chazan & Gordon 1990, p.27)

Some students need step-by-step guidance when becoming familiar with a new procedure for generating questions, gathering information, or carrying out a cooperative task; others, and most students over time, need a reminder of the "big picture." They need considerable discussion in the early stages of a new activity, less when their investigation is well under way.

Getting Help with Individual Learning Needs

Although the kinds of inquiry learning these programs foster is appropriate for all students, many students need special support to manage the social and intellectual challenges of posing and exploring their own questions and in sustaining attention and involvement in long-term projects. EDC's Problem Solving in Science project found that students with even mild learning problems may need considerable coaching in computer-based cooperative learning activities.

This issue was highlighted in observations of a fifth-grade class using *Voyage of the Mimi*, taught by a highly experienced science specialist who had introduced the program to many teachers in his district (Morocco & Dalton 1990). EDC observers followed a bright boy, Max, who had a high interest in science but some learning difficulties, through the several-week unit. Max easily learned the navigation skills and software procedures but was unable to sustain the level of cooperation required by the course. Rigidly critical of the ways members of his group used their navigation tools, Max disrupted their work and wandered in the room a good deal. More than once, he would seize a tool from another student's hands as he was plotting coordinates, with "You can't do it that way!" Despite good ideas and skills, he was gradually excluded from the cooperative activities by his exasperated peers.

In that same classroom, the research team followed another boy with learning difficulties. Aaron managed to mask his lack of understanding of basic navigation concepts with an amiable and attentive manner. However, he let the others in his group make most of the navigation decisions while he looked on. When Aaron finally had to take a turn at the keyboard in a computer simulation requiring that students apply navigation skills to locating and saving a whale, the other students usually directed him through his confusion. In one competition, a girl in his group placed her fingers over his on the keyboard to help him select the correct commands, so that their group would not fall behind the others.

In a hands-on performance assessment by EDC staff at the end of the unit, Max showed that he knew the navigation games perfectly—although the other students would no longer play with him. Aaron was totally unable to manage the computer procedures and did not know the underlying navigation concepts. Viewing videotapes of the performance assessments, the teacher was astonished at Max's social difficulties and at Aaron's total lack of grasp of the navigation material (Morocco & Dalton 1990). The challenges for the teacher were sobering, knowing what students are actually learning in this kind of complex learning environment and providing the different kinds of support required, particularly with several groups engaged in cooperative learning activities.

These cases and other research reports point up the subtle variation in the learning strengths and needs students bring to computer-supported inquiry learning. They point to the challenge for teachers of assessing students' learning in a complex, simulated learning environment (see Chapter IV for a further discussion of assessment). In all of these programs, there are multiple student learning outcomes at stake: acquiring new information, posing "researchable" questions, linking visual and print information, developing specialized computer skills—for working with databases or computer games, cooperative abilities, reasoning and problem-solving abilities. Clearly, teachers need multiple assessment techniques and associated intervention strategies to meet varied student needs.

Within the classroom, close monitoring of students' learning can enable all students to benefit from reform-oriented learning activities. Beyond the classroom, particularly in middle and high schools that are in transition from traditional approaches to more inquiry-oriented approaches, students may need help in making sense of the differences in their experiences and their teachers' expectations across their learning settings.

Integrating Technology-Supported Inquiry Learning with the Larger School Experience

Many students' first experience with technology-supported inquiry learning is an isolated one—as part of a pilot project, a new program, or an individual teacher's experimentation. Until school reform makes this a more pervasive learning environment for students, they may experience a discrepancy between their inquiry learning experiences and the emphasis on factual memorization in other classrooms. Students in the *Geometric Supposer* research project expressed this dissonance and isolation in comments like "I feel so strange. We're the only class..." and "We can't even associate with other kids in the other classes. We're completely different" (Yerushalmy, Chazan & Gordon 1990, pp. 26-27). When discrepancies in philosophy and approach across classrooms are made explicit, particularly at the middle and high school levels, students are more able to adapt to these discrepancies. Their resulting awareness of the ways they are learning can help them to generalize new inquiry skills to new, appropriate situations.

Chapter IV
Support for Teacher Functions

Capabilities Supported by Technology

Technology supports teacher functions that are fundamental if teachers are to provide authentic, active learning experiences as envisioned by education reform goals. These functions include developing and tailoring instructional materials, conducting ongoing assessment of student learning, expanding teachers' content and instructional knowledge, and communicating with parents. In addition to being necessary for providing the kind of learning experiences described in Chapter I, these functions constitute important aspects of the professionalization of teachers, another goal of education reform.

Develop and Tailor Instructional Materials

In inquiry-based environments, students pursue different questions, work at different speeds, use a variety of materials, engage in different activities, and work in flexible groupings. Teachers are increasingly able to draw on technology resources to develop and tailor instructional materials to better meet individual student needs. Two different ways in which teachers can work with technology to provide appropriately tailored instruction are described below.

Creating Technology-Based Instructional Materials—Technology that enables teachers to invent their own materials can be immensely attractive. Teachers in the Saddleback Valley Unified School District in California participated in a hypermedia project whose original intent was to train them to incorporate existing hypermedia stacks into their curriculum (Smith, Chlebicki & Hartman 1991). Once the teachers recognized the limited availability of appropriate hypermedia stacks, however, they asked for training on how to write their own interactive stacks. By the end of the first year of the project, the teachers had received 36 hours of paid training and 4 days of release time. They were able to create 65 original hypermedia stacks along with corresponding lesson plans. This significant support for teacher training—30 percent of the project budget—was an important factor in the teachers' confidence and success with this new technology application.

During the second year of the project, each teacher developed another new hypermedia stack and lesson plan and served as the mentor for another teacher in using existing hypermedia lessons. Given support and time, many teachers would enjoy the challenge of developing their own curriculum materials. Not all teachers would welcome the activity, however, and certainly teachers and administrators want to avoid expending time and money to needlessly "reinvent the wheel." An alternative way of involving teachers in developing technology-based instructional materials is described below.

Modifying Existing Materials—When Judy Jones, a biology teacher in Chapel Hill, North Carolina, began using *Catlab*, a simulation of trait inheritance in cats, for her unit on heredity she found that the activity suggestions that accompanied the software were too open-ended for her students. Because she valued the software's simulation environment, she decided to keep using the software but to modify the procedures for her students, developing four levels of activities that would allow them to acquire the concepts and skills more gradually.

The first activity level began with a very structured simulation in which the students "mated" cats who differed in only one trait. The next two activity levels involved cats who differed in two and three traits. Jones also developed "hint cards" for students who were having difficulty. The final activity level involved looking at statistics on a variety of cat traits and determining how this inheritance pattern could have happened. These activities moved along a spectrum from very structured to open-ended, with the final activity requiring the most independent and creative problem solving.

Hearing of the teacher's invention, the author of the *Catlab* program obtained her permission to incorporate those activities in the software package. As a result, Judy Jones' activities are now distributed with every copy of *Catlab*.

Ideally, teachers and students would be involved in the development and field testing of educational software, but this is not always the case. Moreover, software that has been carefully tested and adapted to one group of students may not work well with students who are younger, have less background knowledge or less familiarity with computers, or have certain learning difficulties. Teachers would like to be able to adapt instructional materials to meet the needs of their particular students. Few teachers have programming skills, however, so the provision of tools to make it easy to extend and modify instructional software is very desirable. Although very feasible technically, this kind of capability is rarely built into commercial materials.

Support Ongoing Assessment

The discussion of individual student learning needs above points up the need for ongoing teacher assessment of students' inquiry learning process. Technology can support the assessment of student work in ways that are useful for guiding instruction. Specifically, technology facilitates (1) obtaining a trace of student thinking processes, (2) collecting real-time feedback from multiple students, (3) storing and retrieving student work and associated comments, and (4) setting individual goals and managing instruction.

Create Trace of Student Learning Processes—Collins, Hawkins, and Frederiksen (1991) assert that appropriate technologies have a strong role to play in tracking the process of learning and thinking by

- Recording how students learn with feedback in novel situations.

- Recording students' thinking and strategic processes by tracing the process by which students maneuver through a problem or task.

- Recording students' abilities to deal with realistic situations.

Earlier technology (the *Mimi* is an example) did not have built-in ways to monitor or track students' progress, making it difficult for teachers to follow the actual learning process, especially for students with learning difficulties (Hawkins & Sheingold 1985; Morocco & Dalton 1990). To assess student learning of navigation skills for the *Mimi* cases, Education Development Corporation designed a hands-on "performance assessment"—placing students individually at the computer with a researcher who took on the role of clinical interviewer as the student played the navigation game individually that is usually played collaboratively with other students. This approach is one model for teacher assessment of individual student learning in a computer-based environment.

An alternative approach is made possible by recent *HyperCard* environments that have the capability to gather a "dribble file" of all of the students' activity in the environment. This file can be placed in a student's portfolio along with the student's visual and writing products. The teacher can examine the file in order to discern the blind alleys, alternative designs, and way of proceeding that characterized the student's efforts. Thus, more powerful technologies provide the capability of obtaining a "trace" of each student's thinking as he or she tackles problems.

In addition to supporting post hoc analyses of student performance, the increased visibility of work on a computer screen, as opposed to the more private nature of paper-and-pencil work, increases the likelihood that teachers will engage in informal, ongoing assessment as students are working (Morocco, Dalton & Tivnan 1989; 1992). As the teacher circulates in the computer lab or in the classroom, it is easy to stop, observe, and intervene while the student is working on an assignment or project. Hawkins and Sheingold (1985) found that teachers noticed more about the way their students were learning as they circulated among students working at computers. One teacher explained,

> I learn a lot more about the individual learning needs of my students because I can watch them learn. Previously, when I was in the teacher-centered mode, I really couldn't watch them learn because I was busy delivering the curriculum. So my role has changed that way—being able to learn a lot more about my students because of computers. (Wiske et al. 1988, p. 38)

Video technologies provide another means for recording and tracking student learning processes. For example, teachers at Skyline Elementary, a Model Technology School in California, have used video equipment (a MicroMacro Lab with table-mounted cameras attached to widescreen video) as a tool for observing and analyzing the strategies used by young children engaged in mathematical problem solving with manipulatives. While videocameras lack the diagnostic and summarizing capabilities of intelligent computer systems, they provide a rich source of data for examining learning processes in action.

Provide Contexts for Authentic Assessment—Technology can be used to present authentic tasks in a standardized manner, thus providing a context for assessing advanced skills. An ongoing SRI project, for example, is using videotaped problem contexts as a vehicle for assessing students' understanding of mathematical problem solving. Each video episode in this *Becoming a Problem Solver* series presents two child actors engaged in an extended effort to solve an interesting, real-life problem. Accompanying the episodes are paper-and-pencil instruments and open-ended questions to help teachers get at students' beliefs about problems (e.g., Can there be more than one right answer?). The teacher's guide provides similar problems for classroom use and suggestions for classroom discussions regarding the strengths and weaknesses of the problem-solving approaches illustrated in the videos.

Real-Time Feedback from Multiple Students—A well-known problem in many conventional classrooms is the mismatch between the level of presentation and the understanding of many students. As teachers describe concepts and procedures, they depend on student feedback to indicate any comprehension problems. Unfortunately, the students who understand the material best are most likely to contribute to class discussion. Students who don't understand simply remain silent, and the instructor continues with an explanation that some students find incomprehensible.

Technology can help ameliorate this problem by providing an instructor with real-time feedback from all the students in a class. At the Saturn School in Minneapolis, teachers use an application for networked computers called the *Discourse System* to facilitate interactive group-based instruction (Bennett & King 1991; Bremer 1991; Hopkins 1991). All the computers in a room are networked to the teacher's computer so that a teacher or a student can present information to the class and then request a response from each student. Every student's response appears in small text windows on the presenter's screen. By using the *Discourse System*, the teacher or presenter can get frequent feedback from all students at one time, as opposed to calling on one student at a time. As a result, the teacher can adjust his or her instruction on the basis of students' responses and can see which students are having difficulty.

Store and Retrieve Student Work and Associated Comments—The issue of assessing and meeting individual student needs in a simulated environment, where students are constructing knowledge over time through a variety of experiences, was a critical one in the immigration project described earlier (Walters & Gardner 1991). In a revised version of *Immigrant 1850*, researchers included an extensive chapter on how to assess student writing by providing guidelines for assessment along with samples of student work to exemplify those guidelines. Some teachers, particularly language arts teachers, found these to be extremely helpful, while others found them cumbersome. After further analysis, the research and development team determined that the development of separate assessments of writing, speaking, and drawing was counterproductive and that what was needed was a way to evaluate the student's whole learning experience This has led to their developing guidelines for developing and assessing portfolios, which are collections of student work produced over a period of time. Portfolios include drafts and plans, as well as final products, commentary, and reflection.

Until recently, no technology provided a comprehensive system for inputting, storing, retrieving, analyzing, and representing performance data. There has been a dearth of support for the teacher to create a systematic database on children's progress over time. In the area of writing, for example, where multiple thinking, language, and composing abilities are developing over time, teachers spend large amounts of time reviewing and commenting on student compositions, but these comments are generally lost from the system once the student has taken them home. The teacher has had no way of storing a history of changing comments on the student's work, or of easily rounding up pointed examples of writing strengths and problems to use for teaching material in the classroom.

Technology currently under development at Education Development Center by Midian Kurland will substantially enhance the teacher's ability to respond to, store, retrieve, assess, and manipulate student work (Kurland 1991). This tool, *TextBrowser*, provides an electronic analogue to teachers' traditional methods for keeping track of assignments, marking student papers, providing feedback, and recording and monitoring student performance, but uses the power of the technology to vastly increase the extent and flexibility with which the teacher can accomplish those tasks. *TextBrowser* enables teachers to access anything a student writes on a computer, review the text, and mark and comment on the text (an electronic "red pen") . The tool maintains a database archive of every text linked with the teacher's annotations and comments, so that portfolios of student work can be created and analyzed. Comments and annotations are automatically entered into an electronic grade book.

The teacher can use the stored information to further analyze student work or create tables, graphs, or summaries of patterns and trends for each student. For example, the teacher could access all examples of a student's work that were marked "needs reorganization." In addition, the teacher can create custom writing exercises from the student's own work. *TextBrowser* can extract text units that meet specified criteria, such as a list of all words the student misspelled during the past week.

This tool supports and enhances the teacher's ability to use electronic writing tools in the classroom, giving the teacher the capability to store and manipulate an assignment so that it can be systematically reviewed, compared against previous work, or used for custom-designed writing exercises. Although *TextBrowser* originated as a system for writing assessment, it can be adapted to assessment in any content area. Kurland has said that critical issues in the effective use of this tool are teacher knowledge about the process approach to teaching writing, children's development of writing abilities, and the particular abilities and needs of individual children. Presumably, comparable requirements will hold as the tool is extended into other content areas (Kurland 1991).

Set Goals and Manage Instruction—Teaching involves a great deal of management of student instructional goals and performance records, especially when instruction is individualized. One of the biggest draws for integrated learning systems has been their inclusion of software to automate this process. Each student's learning objectives, units attempted and completed, and performance on end-of-module assessments are recorded. Many systems are able to generate reports of both individual and whole-class performance. It is possible to obtain these same instructional management features apart from an integrated learning system for instructional delivery.

Technology is supporting a particularly sophisticated system for instructional management at the Saturn School. Teachers are using technology to respond to, store, and manipulate complex student performance data. Each student has a Personal Growth Plan (PGP), consisting of goals negotiated with staff and parents but written in the student's own words (Bennett & King 1991). This plan is stored on both teacher- and student-accessible networks, where students and teachers can set goals and track student accomplishments.

The student or teacher can query the system for learning activities (e.g., courses, workshops, community volunteer opportunities, mentorship programs) relevant to a particular goal. The system uses a keyword search strategy coupled with a data bank to provide this information. Students can insert changes and revise their goals (after negotiation with their advisor), and the system supports reflection on their growth and development relative to their goals. Each student in the school has a portfolio of proficiencies, which is compiled throughout the student's years in the school. There are pop-up windows for teacher comments and notes regarding the student's activities and goals. The student's portfolio includes both hard copy and items that are stored electronically on the network, including text files, *HyperCard* stacks, and videos. As a result, both students and teachers are able to easily retrieve and review work from the current or previous year.

Taken altogether, the various components of the system developed and used at Saturn school provide an interesting example of how technology can support a comprehensive, integrated approach to instructional management. A key feature of the system is the opportunity it provides for students to take an active role in managing and negotiating their own learning experiences (through goal-setting, identifying key learning opportunities, responding to feedback, and recording and evaluating their progress).

Share and Expand Teacher Knowledge

Telecommunication systems are helping teachers break out of their traditional isolation to connect with colleagues and professionals in distant locations. These interactions can help teachers develop a clearer image of effective teaching and learning environments, understand how technology enables them to create these environments, learn about effective instructional strategies, share information about students, and gain emotional support for change. Telecommunications enables the teacher to be in frequent communication with people outside of the classroom with no disruption of class activities. The teacher is not interrupted by a phone call; rather, the message waits until the teacher is ready to receive it. Participation in a telecommunications network can help a teacher develop new instructional strategies that promote inquiry learning.

Interaction with Colleagues—One of the most frustrating features of the teacher's job is the paucity of opportunities to interact with colleagues in working on the central problems of curriculum and instruction. The opportunity for teachers to work cooperatively with other teachers is considered a crucial program ingredient in the AT&T Learning Network described previously. According to Riel (1990b), "Teachers cannot be expected to reorganize classrooms to provide [a cooperative learning environment] for students while they themselves remain in the isolation of the traditional classroom" (p. 464). If teachers are engaged in cooperation and collaboration with their professional peers, it will be more natural for them to provide the same sort of environment for their students.

Beyond providing an avenue for communication about cooperative projects, the AT&T Learning Network provides a forum for this more in-depth and reflective communication between professionals. The learning circle projects have provided teachers with an opening through which they can communicate with each other. Riel (1990b) found that teachers who were part of the AT&T learning circles asked each other for suggestions and advice and thus gained new ideas about classroom organization and teaching practices. They also learned from one another by reading descriptions of events taking place in other classrooms. As teachers share descriptions of things happening in their own classrooms, other teachers may adopt some of those ideas.

The way in which technology can support this collegial process is illustrated by the extended electronic conversation conducted among teachers in one learning circle in response to a teacher's query about portfolio assessment. Larry Adamson, a learning circle coordinator, sent the following message to the teachers on his circle:

> So you want to talk about portfolios!!! One of my favorite topics. I've been using some form of portfolio evaluation over the last four years. What I'm really into is all forms of authentic assessment. I agree with Nancy's comment about "dittos and tests," there is a better way to evaluate. Exactly what the "way" should be is still being widely debated.

The following week, after some other participants reacted to his comments and asked for more information, Adamson continued his discussion of portfolio assessment:

I also use traditional writing folders, which is a primitive form of a portfolio. I have my students write 15 to 20 minutes every night for homework, and when they come into my class I simply stamp their work and have them save it in their binders. ... Through binders, writing folders, portfolios, holistic assessment, writing workshop, and individual conferencing, I'm able to get a pretty good grasp of an individual student's strengths and weaknesses, and I have evidence to support my evaluation....

As I mentioned earlier, this is also one of the reasons I like working on the AT&T Learning Network. It gives me an opportunity to see what student writing looks like around the world. It gives my students an opportunity to compare their writing with other students their same age. It has really worked as a motivator for me. If I publish a piece of student writing on the Network they get extra credit and it is included in their portfolio. I try to make it as much like the real world of publishing as I can.

He asked others to send more messages about what they were doing:

Margaret...I'd also be interested in hearing more about what your district is doing to formalize the portfolio process. Jo and Angelo, what are your thoughts on portfolios?

Two weeks later, Angelo Abby responded to Adamson's query:

Anyway, on to portfolios. I am reading with fascination the many conversations that have taken place concerning this new/old technique for keeping track of a student's progress. We have been talking about this idea for the past few weeks on the assessment committee, of which I am a part. We are trying to find information about what other schools have done along the portfolio line and the network has supplied me with some material to share with my colleagues. I really have enjoyed hearing the pros/cons about the idea and have passed along the info to people in my building.

When the teachers participating in the AT&T Learning Network were asked about the benefits of educational electronic networking, most rated *their own learning*, not the learning of their students, as the most important benefit of the program (Riel 1990b). The network changed and improved the working conditions for teachers, enabling them to communicate and share ideas with other professionals. As Angelo Abby wrote, "... this collaboration is wonderful. I didn't have to make telephone calls to anyone, or leave my building to find out the information I needed. I sat at the computer and discovered that my problem was already on the network." A week later, he continued: "I have truly enjoyed the eavesdropping that I feel I have done for the past few months reading such good material from all of you. Your comments to Margaret Riel about collaboration, your ideas about portfolios, your feelings about telecommunications—all have been absorbed by me as well as several of my peers (anyone who would listen, as a matter of fact)." Larry Adamson commented, "relationships seem to be forming all over the network. I have a feeling that this is only the beginning. We are the nucleus of what may develop into a worldwide faculty."

Research on the AT&T Learning Network suggests that participation in the learning circles increased teachers' self-esteem as well as their knowledge (Riel 1990b). Network interaction can "open a small window on classroom activities" (p. 457) so that teachers receive recognition and praise from their peers. For example, transcripts from the network show how teachers who were already using portfolio assessment received special praise and recognition from other teachers who were struggling to begin what seemed like an overwhelming task. When teachers select projects for the Learning Network, they are often showcasing some of their best lessons and receive much positive feedback from their circle partners. There is also a recognition among teachers that "skilled performances by students usually mark skilled performances by their teachers" (p. 458), and the teachers receive a great deal of positive feedback in that respect. Also, when teachers see their ideas being adapted or evolving in other classrooms in distant locations, it is extremely exciting and rewarding.

All of these opportunities for feedback and praise from peers in distant locations increase teachers' excitement about the learning project. And when teachers get excited about learning, "their students share their teachers' enthusiasm and the quality of the students' work increases" (p. 459).

Access to Subject Matter Experts—In addition to providing links to colleagues, technology can give teachers access to experts in the subject matter they are trying to teach. Even the best-prepared teacher cannot know everything in a given field, and knowledge about new developments is by definition vested in just a few individuals. With technology comes the power to have increasing access to subject matter experts, giving teachers the opportunity to strengthen their knowledge of the content areas they teach.

An example of this trend is the Urban Math Collaborative (UMC), which links teachers and university mathematicians in order to deepen teachers' knowledge of mathematics and to help them respond to emerging new standards in the mathematics education community. Discussions on the electronic network of the UMC have deepened teachers' content knowledge and have also touched on teaching issues that do not get dealt with as openly and meaningfully in other forums. Discussions are often more in-depth and reflective, since comments and opinions that are shared on the network are addressed to a potentially wide audience and tend to be more carefully thought through than those offered in more casual, face-to-face settings (Driscoll & Kelemanik 1991).

Support Communication with Parents

Voice Link services, provided to over two dozen Connecticut towns by the Southern New England Telecommunications Corporation, allow teachers to inform parents about homework, report cards, and field trips (Douglas & Bransford 1991). Something as simple as having a telephone in the classroom can free the teacher from security concerns and can be a readily available channel between teachers and parents. Voicemail to update parents on material covered in class and on homework and voice bulletin boards to post school activities can keep students, parents, and the community informed about the activities of the school (Heller 1991). Using current telephone technologies, several communities have already established "Homework Hotline" or "Dial a Teacher" programs.

Such programs have only begun to explore the ways in which technology could help parents become more involved in their students' learning, however. Lesgold et al. (1992) envision a time when emerging wider-bandwidth networks make it possible for parents to get much more than a listing of required homework exercises: teachers might include notes about the goals of each lesson, background information, and suggested enrichment activities. Parents could use this information as a starting point for engaging their children in related learning activities. They would also have a medium for ongoing discussions of their children's progress and learning needs.

Challenges for Teachers Using Technology

When teachers use technology as a critical part of an inquiry-oriented learning-teaching process, they face a set of challenges, including

- Learning how to use a variety of technology applications;

- Using, adapting, and designing technology-enhanced curricula to meet students' needs;

- Expanding content knowledge;

- Taking on new roles; and

- Responding to individual students.

None of these challenges stand alone; they are tightly interrelated. We discuss each challenge below.

Learning How to Use a Variety of Technology Options

When we think of teachers learning to use a variety of technology applications, we tend to focus primarily on their need to learn how to operate hardware and software. Although this is a critical component, teachers also need to develop a method of keeping abreast of new technologies and finding out about the potential power each technology application has with respect to inquiry-based teaching and learning. Each new application brings new benefits and new problems to be solved.

For example, although electronic networks are opening the classroom to new learning for both teachers and students, this medium brings new challenges for teachers. Driscoll and Kelemanik (1991) have found that it is very difficult for teachers to sustain regular, substantive discussions on a network. The discontinuity in conversation can be a big disadvantage because if some questions go unanswered, a request is ignored, or interesting lines of discussion are not pursued, the conversation may falter and users may drop out. Riel (1990a) has found that the use of bulletin boards is very time-consuming and that it is sometimes inefficient for teachers to negotiate their way through these bulletin boards in search of applicable and appropriate ideas or conversations.

In response to this problem, one junior high school in Maine hired a part-time computer network coordinator who monitors 11 different conferences on the PSINET network. The coordinator prints out the mail, reads through it, and sends copies to the teachers or administrators in the district for whom the information is useful. Occasionally, teachers will request particular information, and the network coordinator will send that request to the appropriate conference on the network (Ray 1991).

As teachers become more knowledgeable about the technology applications that are available, they need to develop criteria for selecting the applications that would be most valuable and effective, given the context of their class and student needs. They also need information that allows them to make wise decisions about allocating resources among students and managing instruction within the classroom. These decisions are closely tied to curriculum issues.

Using, Adapting and Designing Technology-Enhanced Curricula

When teachers integrate technology applications into the curriculum, they knowingly or unknowingly are curriculum developers. The programs discussed above and in Chapter III reflect three different models for integrating technology into inquiry-oriented curricula. In one model, teachers may find a particularly exciting technology application to integrate into existing instruction (e.g., *Catlab*). Room is made within the curriculum to accommodate this application. In another model, the teacher accesses a complete and comprehensive multimedia curriculum (e.g., *Voyage of the Mimi*). From the rich array of available resources, the teacher must select and sequence those she or he wants to use. In a third model, teachers construct a curriculum unit around a theme or topic, using a variety of technology applications (e.g., the construction of an I-Search unit in *MAKE IT HAPPEN!*).

Regardless of how extensively technology is used (one program or multiple programs) or how state of the art the technology applications being used might be (word processing, laser disc, CD-ROM), any technology integration requires that teachers engage in rethinking, reshifting, and reshaping their curriculum. Any technology use should force teachers to pose questions such as: What does the technology offer my students in terms of developing concepts and content? How does it help them to carry out inquiry processes? How will they work together collaboratively or cooperatively?

What is the relationship between the technology and other instructional materials? What knowledge, processes, skills do students need before using the technology? What new knowledge of my content or discipline, of teaching, or of technology do I need in order to foster new learning in my students? The answers to questions such as these have important implications for teachers' own learning and for their role in the classroom.

Expanding Content Knowledge

Many of the technology applications described above and in Chapter III imply a broader and deeper knowledge of the discipline than may be required by curricula that assume teachers transmit a fixed body of information. After studying teachers' use of *Geometric Supposer* for one school year, Yerushalmy, Chazan, and Gordon (1988) concluded that for the teacher to be successful, he or she must know the subject matter, function as a leader and manager of a community of learners, be flexible, and have time for planning and preparation throughout the year. Similarly, Wiske (1990) concluded from her study of high school teachers who used *Geometric Supposer* that teachers need a deep and wide knowledge of their subject matter and a clear understanding of the process of building mathematical understanding to use the software effectively. To deal deftly with potentially unanticipated ideas, teachers need a detailed map of the geometry territory students might explore. Besides a thorough knowledge of geometry, teachers also need to understand the processes of reasoning inductively and deductively and of integrating knowledge from both sorts of thinking to develop mathematics.

Research findings on *The Voyage of the Mimi* indicate that teachers' science and mathematics background and their preferred teaching style had an impact on what, when, and how they used the materials. Interestingly, the flexibility of the materials and the ability to make decisions about when and how to use particular materials helped teachers grapple with their own limitations in science and mathematics (Martin 1987). Although teachers can learn alongside students, discomfort with the content may cause them to limit students' experiences and explorations.

Taking on New Roles

Although teacher-designed inquiry environments can have enormous motivating power for students, they require advanced skills—in curriculum and instruction, in team building and interdisciplinary curriculum design, as well as in technology—on the part of the teacher. Field-test results of *MAKE IT HAPPEN!* reveal that teachers need to know a good deal about the I-Search process to design and implement these units. Morocco (1991) compared the case studies of the New Hampshire and Massachusetts design teams in the *MAKE IT HAPPEN!* field test to describe the importance of having a facilitator who acts as coach to a new teacher design team as they learn new curriculum design and teaching roles (Zorfass, Morocco & Lory 1991).

These computer-supported inquiry programs also require advanced teacher skills in integrating technology into inquiry learning. Beyond "procedural knowledge" of the software, teachers need "conditional knowledge" of the contexts and situations in which the tools are appropriate and the ability to recognize those situations as they arise. When students are beginning to generate related ideas for their topic, for example, the teacher needs to recognize *at that moment* the contribution a software mapping tool like *Inspiration* might make to students' organizing of ideas.

Teachers using *Geometric Supposer* not only need to learn how to use the software but also must be able to apply it to a variety of teaching-learning situations. Wiske (1990) explained, "Teachers not only had to become familiar with the software, but also needed to develop the skills to use it in a variety of teaching formats; e.g., as a dynamic demonstration tool during class presentations, as an aid during class discussions to illustrate or verify points, and as a part of examinations of students' performance. ... Fluency in one format does not automatically extend to other formats without conscious preparation and practice" (p. 8).

When teachers use and develop inquiry-based curricula that integrate technology, their role in the classroom becomes more that of a coach or facilitator of student learning. In inquiry-based learning, teachers set the context, help students pose questions to explore, stimulate problem solving, and give students tools and resources to use so that they—the students—can construct knowledge. The knowledge construction process takes place within an individual student: it is highly individualistic because of the knowledge maker's prior knowledge, experience, skills, and talent. Knowledge making can follow routes unanticipated by the teacher. For teachers and students to follow these new routes, a curriculum needs to be flexible. Teachers cannot—and should not expect to—have a total grasp of the content related to every topic. What they do need to know is how to help guide students through the meaning-making process: how to ask probing questions, how to connect students to relevant resources, how to organize students into cooperative learning groups, and how to give them tools to store, manipulate, and analyze information.

Although teachers may see the desirability of this type of teaching role, they often feel vulnerable as they take the risk of shifting from a more comfortable knowledge transmission mode of teaching to inquiry-based teaching. One reason for this discomfort is their appreciation of the difficulty of managing meaning-making across a class and within individuals.

Responding to Individual Students

Many technology applications (e.g., *TextBrowser*, word processing, databases) offer teachers a window into the student's thinking, inquiry, and problem-solving processes. When the work students are doing is visible on a monitor or printout, teachers have access to students' misconceptions, the ways in which they sort and categorize information, the relationships they form among ideas, and the conjectures they make. In a teacher's view, a student's response may not be the most logical, appropriate, or even "correct" response. However, trial and error is part of problem solving. Teachers are often tempted to intervene too early or too often, being motivated by their genuine desire to set a student "on the right track" and to avoid floundering. This tendency can be exacerbated by the public character of the computer monitor, which makes the students' work more visible and accessible to intervention by the teacher at all stages compared with the more private medium of paper and pencil. Intervention in students' work at an early stage can be helpful, but it also can thwart students, short-circuiting their own construction of knowledge. Michael Hopkins, the lead teacher at the Saturn School, has had students use technology, such as *HyperCard* presentations, *LEGO Logo* projects, and other multimedia programs to produce projects. He cautions:

> Teachers have to be very careful to honor the learner in these situations. Many times an astute teacher can see an opportunity to show a student a better or more efficient way to proceed. I have found that students would rather not hear about my great idea in the context of their current project. It is often easier for them to hear my idea after the fact, when they have already found a personally satisfying solution. Sometimes the most useful role for the teacher is that of sounding board. Instead of trying to teach students how they should think about a problem, I try to help them understand how they do think about it. (Hopkins 1991, p. 30)

Teachers need to know a great deal about cognitive processes and processing in general and the learning styles and strengths of individual students in particular. When students work collaboratively on a technology-based assignment, teachers face a thorny issue. In the Earth Lab project, for example, teachers can review both individual and group workspaces (Newman 1990a; 1992a). Although teachers need to assess group performance on a project, they also need to tease out evidence of individual performance to help students who may become lost in the dynamics of a group situation.

Conclusion

The initial enthusiasm for technology (especially computers) included rosy predictions about making teachers' jobs easier—with technology performing the curriculum selection, rote correction, and instructional management roles, teachers could devote themselves to the "human side" of teaching. Experience has shown these early predictions to be naive. Teachers are nearly unanimous in concluding that in the early stages of technology implementation, at least, their job becomes harder. The technical demands posed by technology use are just the tip of the iceberg. Teachers must be able to select, adapt, or design technology-enhanced materials that meet the needs of their particular students. Technology-enhanced curricula often place new demands on teachers' subject matter knowledge and nearly always require them to take on new roles as curriculum designer, team builder, and coach. Complex, collaborative technology-based work can make assessing individual students a complex undertaking.

Teachers contemplating the above set of issues might well ask themselves whether their involvement with technology will be worth the trouble. The response from thousands of teachers who have tried it would be a resounding "yes!" Teachers involved in the kinds of activities described in this chapter and the preceding one typically find a new sense of mission and professionalism. They stick with technology, despite the growing pains it causes, because they sense that their students are learning more and approaching their classroom activities with a heightened level of motivation. Moreover, the new skills that the teachers themselves acquire, and the satisfaction of facing a challenge and overcoming it, add to teachers' sense of professional growth.

Although technology poses many challenges for teachers, it also provides powerful tools for supporting the teacher's work. New software makes developing and modifying technology-based materials easier (although there is still much room for improvement). Technology provides a capability to store and manipulate both the products of student work and teacher evaluations. Finally, technology is making it possible for teachers to break out of their traditional isolation, communicating with outside content experts and their peers about the instructional content and pedagogical issues that are the heart of their work, and communicating with parents about expectations, activities, assignments, and student progress.

Chapter V
Effects on Student Achievement

Although an argument can be made for including technology in schooling for its own sake (i.e., to prepare students for the technology-laden environments they will face as adults; see Collins 1990), many policymakers and community members want evidence of the effects of technology on student learning as they make decisions about technology investments. In this chapter, we have not attempted to compile all the studies on this topic. Rather, we have written about a sample of studies, selected to represent the major approaches and issues in the research literature.

"Horse Race" Studies

When a new instructional technology appears on the scene, it is quite natural to want to compare its effectiveness with that of existing technologies. Early studies compared instruction via radio and, later, television, with learning based on classroom lectures or textbooks. More recently, hundreds of studies have been conducted comparing computer-assisted instruction with more traditional modes (Kulik, Bangert & Williams 1983; Samson, Niemiec, Weinstein & Walberg 1986). Smaller bodies of literature exist on interactive videodisc (Bosco 1986) and distance-learning (Moore 1989).

Comparing Technology Media with Conventional Instruction

Most of this literature finds newer technologies to be either equivalent or superior to conventional instruction with regard to student learning (Bialo & Sivin 1990).

Computer-Assisted Instruction—Meta-analyses of studies at the elementary school (Kulik, Kulik & Bangert-Drowns 1984; Niemiec & Walberg 1985) and secondary school (Bangert-Drowns, Kulik & Kulik 1985; Kulik, Bangert & Williams 1983; Samson, Niemiec, Weinstein & Walberg 1986) levels generally show a significant advantage for computer-assisted instruction. Kulik, Kulik, and Bangert-Drowns (1985) found that on average, CAI students at the elementary school level outperform their counterparts without CAI by .47 standard deviations. The comparable estimate for secondary school students is .32 standard deviations (Kulik, Bangert, & Williams 1983). The relative advantage of computer-assisted instruction in these reports appears stronger for younger, disadvantaged, and low-ability students (Bangert-Drowns, Kulik & Kulik 1985; Samson et al. 1986) and for males (Niemiec & Walberg 1985).

When Clark (1985) reexamined samples of the studies included in earlier meta-analyses, however, he found that effect sizes were much smaller when the same teacher provided instruction in both treatment and comparison groups and were absent when instructional method was controlled (such that the study measured the effect of instructional delivery medium only). Effects were larger in shorter-term studies, suggesting that novelty effects boost performance with new technologies in the short term but tend to wear off over time.

Videodisc and Multimedia Technologies—Advantages of interactive videodisc over lectures have been reported (e.g., Nelson, Watson & Busch 1989). Fletcher (1990) conducted a meta-analysis of 47 studies comparing instruction via computer-controlled interactive videodisc (IVD) with conventional instruction in military training, industrial training, and higher education settings. On average, those who learned through IVD had achievement scores that were .50 standard deviation higher than those of students taught conventionally. Bosco (1986) reviewed eight IVD studies conducted in school settings; some of the studies found an advantage for the videodisc presentation, while others reported no significant difference.

Several studies have found positive effects in having students develop their own curriculum materials using hypermedia. When asked to draw "concept maps" of the Enlightenment, eleventh-grade history students who had studied the period using a hypermedia corpus called ACCESS (American Culture in Context: Enrichment for Secondary Schools) had more information within their maps and used more abstract concepts to organize the information they had than did their peers who had not used the hypermedia materials (Spoehr 1992). In research conducted by Richard Lehrer, ninth-grade students were retested a year after they had studied the Civil War, some by developing hypermedia presentations and others through traditional approaches. Those with the hypermedia experience had a more realistic understanding of the role of the historian, recalled more Civil War facts, and had more elaborated concepts (Lehrer, Erickson & Connell 1992).

There are relatively few studies providing evidence regarding the effects of new information storage technologies such as CD-ROM. In one study, the term papers of eighth graders using a computer-based videotex encyclopedia were judged to show greater knowledge than those of students using a print-based encyclopedia (Krendl & Fredin 1985).

Distance-learning—Although there is a voluminous literature on distance-learning, there is very little empirical evidence of effects on student learning (Moore 1989). Because distance-learning is generally implemented in situations in which face-to-face instruction in a particular subject area is either infeasible or more expensive, proponents have sought to show that it is equal to, rather than better than, traditional approaches. An evaluation of a two-way interactive television project in Iowa found that students in television classes performed equivalently to students in other sections of the class taught by the same teacher (Nelson 1985). Similarly, a series of studies of ITV in rural Minnesota found no significant achievement differences when students were compared with those in conventional classes (Kitchen 1987).

Limitations of the "Horse Race" Paradigm

As logical as this comparative experimental approach seems on first consideration, the methodology and interpretation of these findings are highly problematic. Summarizing findings as showing the effectiveness of "computer-assisted instruction" or "interactive videodisc" or any other delivery medium is clearly misleading. When an innovation is tried, it necessarily includes not just a given technology medium (i.e., computers or television or books) but also particular instructional content and methods (as represented in the software or programming or text). These variables will interact with features of the context within which the innovation is used and with the characteristics of the particular students involved. When differences are found, there is no defensible logic to attributing them to a technology medium rather than to instructional content or method, instructor or student characteristics, or some interaction among these variables.

As Clark (1985) points out, if you really want to assess the comparative effectiveness of the technology medium per se, you need to hold everything else constant. When Clark reexamined a sample of the CAI studies reviewed in earlier meta-analyses, he found that instructional method was equated in only half of the comparison studies. When those studies using the same instructional approach in both groups were analyzed separately, there was no effect of presenting the instruction via computer.

It is not clear, however, that the purity of experimental design espoused by Clark would prove very useful for policy-oriented research. To hold everything constant except the medium used to deliver instruction, studies have to sacrifice representativeness, looking at only a very circumscribed piece of content taught by the new technology and through a more traditional medium (e.g., lecture or textbook). Thus, for example, if a teacher designs a special lesson using specific instructional objectives, diagnostic routines, branching rules, and feedback patterned after those used in a CAI program, and we find that students in her classes perform equivalently to those using CAI, what does this tell us about the effectiveness of CAI compared with typical classroom teaching?

On reflection, in most cases, we are really not interested in whether or not there are effects of the delivery medium per se. We almost never implement a change in medium only. Particularly when we want to understand how technology can support education reform, *we want to change the content and the instructional strategy as well as the medium*. In such cases, we need to look at specific effects of various facets of the innovation and at the implementation process and how students and teachers use technology, rather than simply comparing two different delivery media in terms of a single outcome measure.

On the dependent-variable side, issues can be equally thorny. Many studies, particularly those examining longer interventions, compare treatments in terms of outcomes on standardized tests. Because the treatment conditions are rarely equated in terms of instructional content, the tests that are used as learner outcome measures are usually more congruent with the objectives and content of one treatment than with those of the other. Thus, the comparison is inherently unfair. Because the tests are usually multiple-choice measures of basic skills, those applications that are most similar to the tests (e.g., drill and practice in basic skills) have tended to show the largest gains (Bangert-Drowns, Kulik & Kulik 1985). A comparable bias may exist in those studies that have designed their own learner outcome measures around the content and presentation format used in the new technology (Samson, Niemiec, Weinstein & Walberg 1986). Students taught different content by a different approach would not be expected to do as well on these measures, regardless of the medium used to deliver the instruction.

The accumulation of comparative studies biased in their choice of control groups or outcome measures does little to help us understand what features of the treatment are critical for producing the desired effects. Although still common in the evaluation literature, these studies are being superseded by more elaborate approaches, as discussed below.

Contextualized Research

Concerns over the limitations of "horse race" studies, such as those expressed above, have led to a new approach to measuring the effects of technology-based innovations on student learning. Recognizing that student performance will be affected not just by hardware and software but also by the way a particular class or student uses the technology and the culture of the classroom, these studies have supplied detailed descriptions of specific implementations. Salomon (1991) has made the case for this kind of research:

> Say, we had one classroom with teamwork at the computers and another without. Still, we could not assume that the two classrooms were identical save for the presence or absence of teamwork. Everything would be different.... The underlying assumption here is that classroom events are tied to each other in a systemic way. That is, that each component, event, or action has the potential of affecting the unit as a whole; the whole is assumed to be more than the sum of its components and is characterized by the patterns and forms of the relations among them.... Clearly, one could not answer the question of how much did the computer, or any other event, contribute to the outcomes. It would be like asking how much did the flute, in a 120-piece orchestra, contribute to the quality of the music.... Alternatively, one would want to use a methodology that respects the systemic nature of the classroom, the way this system differs from its controls, and the way it changes over time. The emphasis ought not to be on single events or variables but on the way they relate to each other. (pp. 13-14)

This approach to studying the effects of technology-based innovations focuses on understanding the relationships among various elements in the project, and the variables that contribute to specific outcomes, rather than to declare the innovation as more or less effective than some other approach.

Ann Brown (1992) describes the way in which her involvement with complex classroom-based innovations has led to a widening of the methodologies she uses in her research. She and her colleagues have been studying sixth-, seventh-, and eighth-grade science classes in inner-city schools. In the experimental classes, teachers and researchers have attempted to create a "community of learners," in which students are involved in inquiry-based learning, supported by multimedia technology (Brown, Ash, Rutherford,

Nakagawa, Gordon & Campione, in press). Students create part of their own curriculum. Given a specific subtopic, a small group prepares hypermedia study materials on that topic. Students are then regrouped for learning in such a way that each of the new groups contains one student who worked on the curriculum materials for each topic. Each student functions as a discussion leader when the study group moves to the topic of his or her expertise. Assessment of the effects of the innovation includes administering standard pretest and posttest measures to all students.

The significant improvement of the experimental classes on these measures (in absolute terms and relative to control classes) suggests that there are gains worthy of understanding (Brown 1992). Such analyses are only a small part of the research, however; Brown and her colleagues perform detailed case studies on the conceptual growth of individual students in order to understand and to illustrate the nature of the phenomena that appear to be responsible for the observed gains (e.g., the acquisition of specific biological principles contrasted with memorization of specific facts).

Another example of contextualized research is provided by Riel (1989), who described what happened in four classes of San Diego fourth graders who participated with students in Hawaii, Mexico, and Alaska in an on-line "newswire" service and production of a student newspaper. Students in all four classes showed an improvement of more than one grade level in their reading and writing skills. Those students who served as volunteer editors showed striking gains in language mechanics. Riel's observations led her to conclude that the experience of editing others' writing produces more improvement than practice correcting one's own mistakes and that students are reluctant to edit the work of their classmates but much freer to criticize and correct the work of a distant peer.

A second study, examining the quality of writing of Israeli seventh graders participating in a similar intercultural student network, provides further evidence of the educational value of these activities. Half of the students were instructed to write an article for their teacher to determine their semester grade; the other half were told to compose an article for their distant peers on the network. Judges who were blind to each student author's condition rated the resulting articles. Writing produced for peers was judged as significantly better than that produced for a grade: the content was more substantive, there were more supporting details, less slang, more complex constructions, and fewer mechanical errors.

Another example of contextualized research on technology in the classroom is provided by researchers at the Ontario Institute for Studies in Education (OISE) who have developed a networked hypermedia system called Computer-Supported Intentional Learning Environments (CSILE). CSILE uses a central database and provides capabilities for students to write, illustrate, read, and comment on the information in the system (Scardamalia, Bereiter, McLean, Swallow & Woodruff 1989). It is being used with elementary school classes as they study science, history, and social studies. The system is designed to be used collaboratively, with students accessing each other's work and making their own notations, supplying critiques, additional information, and other types of help. The author of the material being commented on is notified, setting the stage for students to engage in interchange concerning the material they are studying.

One of the research issues being addressed is the extent to which students of different ability levels participate in this kind of instructional activity. OISE is finding that students at all ability levels participate equally and interact effectively with CSILE (Bryson & Scardamalia 1991). In fact, in classrooms that implement the model in the most collaborative fashion, the advantages of CSILE use are particularly strong among the lower- and middle-ability groups.

A final noteworthy example of contextualized research on student learning outcomes is provided by the evaluation under way for the *Jasper* videodisc series described earlier. *Jasper* adventures are being used on an experimental basis in 52 classes in 9 states (Pellegrino et al. 1992). Each class is supported by a representative from a corporation that is contributing to the project. Participating teachers receive 2 weeks of training in a summer workshop. In the first years of implementation, teachers have varied in the degree to which they are comfortable turning control of the problem-solving activities over to groups of students.

Nevertheless, as a whole, classrooms using *Jasper* videodiscs show significant advantages—over control group classrooms matched in demographic characteristics—in terms of student attitudes toward mathematics, mathematical concepts, and ability to plan their problem solving (Pellegrino et al. 1992). Embedded research studies are examining the effects of factors such as working in two-person teams versus individually (Barron & Rieser 1992).

It should be noted that these contextualized studies, which provide much more detail than is summarized here, seek to understand the complex interplay between an innovation, which is itself an amalgamation of many instructional features, and the particular culture of a classroom or characteristics of individual students. Although the discussion above focuses on effects on measures of student learning of achievement, one of the hallmarks of contextualized studies is their investigation of the variables that may mediate between the introduction of technology and student learning. Considered as a whole, there are now enough studies of technology within an instructional framework emphasizing work on challenging tasks to suggest that this approach can bring about a transformation of the classroom. Researchers report a shift from teacher-led activities to student-centered learning, including an increase of collaborative learning (Collins 1990). Students are typically described as more engaged and highly motivated (Dwyer, Ringstaff & Sandholtz 1990). Teacher behavior is described as less didactic and more coach-like (Collins 1990). Many teachers report being able to explore more complex topics with the aid of computers than they could with their earlier approaches (Sheingold & Hadley 1990).

Thus, it seems clear that, when used as part of an instructional approach involving students in complex, authentic tasks, technology can support the kind of transformation of student learning that is at the heart of education reform.

Contextualized studies are not designed to be summarized in terms of quantitative measures of effect size and are not conducive to the meta-analytic techniques used with the comparative "horse race" studies. Nevertheless, it may encourage policymakers to note that positive effects relative to control classrooms have been reported by Brown (1992), the *Jasper* project (Pellegrino et al. 1992), and the CSILE project (Bryson & Scardamalia 1991).

The studies summarized above provide examples of the kind of encouraging results that are being observed in individual projects. There is a need for many more such projects, however, to provide the data needed for the kind of theory-based research synthesis the field needs (Herman 1992). In addition, many of the projects described above have benefited from the active, intense involvement of researchers; the extent to which these successes can be replicated within the existing educational system remains to be demonstrated.

Experimental Studies

Salomon (1991) argues that the advancement of education research requires both systemic studies, a concept similar to what we have called contextualized research above, and analytic studies. The latter are carefully designed experiments used to investigate the relationship between a particular feature of a technology innovation (e.g., a particular way of presenting a navigation concept) and a logically related aspect of student performance (e.g., number of times students use the concept in figuring the fastest route in novel map problems).

These studies lack the ecological validity or representativeness of the contextualized research described above, but they are a powerful aid in helping to derive design principles for constructing new applications. These studies differ from the "horse race" studies described earlier in that they do not try to compare two complicated combinations of technology, content, and instructional methods but rather to relate a specific feature of a technology to a specific outcome.

This kind of research can be illustrated with experimental studies of microcomputer-based laboratories (MBLs). As described earlier, MBLs combine a microcomputer-based program for graphing analog data with a set of external measurement devices (e.g., motion sensors, temperature probes) that can be used to collect the data. Previous research had found that junior high school students often misinterpret graphs, confusing the depiction of absolute level with the concept of change (slope). Mokros and Tinker (1987) found that students using MBLs reduced this type of error relative to students who collected data and graphed it manually. By comparing conditions in which two groups collected data through MBLs and saw it displayed either in real time or after a 20-second delay, Brasell (1987) was able to show that 90 percent of the improvement of the regular MBL group was dependent on their ability to see the data graphed in real time. Even a delay as brief as 20 seconds appears to seriously disrupt students' ability to see the connection between graphed data and real-world physical events.

Spoehr (1992) followed up her original work on ACCESS with an experimental study contrasting two different versions of the database. She found that giving students a hierarchical structure for the corpus, through overview cards and labeling of the links between nodes, appears critical in producing deeper conceptual understanding of the content under study.

Zellermayer, Salomon, Globerson and Givon (1991) investigated the effects of *Writing Partner*, an interactive computer tool designed to help student writers by providing guidance regarding the metacognitive aspects of writing (e.g., attention to the characteristics of the intended audience). Secondary school students who wrote essays with guidance from this tool subsequently wrote better essays and showed evidence of having internalized the guidance when writing independently (without the computer tool). Students who wrote the same number of essays with regular word processing software or who used a version of *Writing Partner* that gave guidance only when it was requested showed no improvement.

Cost-Effectiveness Studies

One way in which research on educational technologies is increasing in sophistication is to recast the question within a cost–benefit framework. These studies seek to compare the relative cost of attaining a certain level of improvement in student performance through various technologies. Such studies are appealing to policymakers because they deal with the ingredients and variables an administrator can manipulate (e.g., staff, facilities, instructional time). If carefully performed, such studies can be very informative simply by making explicit all of the cost elements going into a particular instructional approach. Some of these are often overlooked. For example, in an analysis of the economics of using CAI delivered through microcomputers, Levin (1989) points out that the ingredients needed may include (1) the time not only of teachers but also of teaching specialists, coordinators, and administrators; (2) physical space for the equipment and whatever security devices, air conditioning, or special wiring is needed; (3) not only the computers themselves but supporting equipment, such as printers, cooling fans, surge protectors, special furnishings, and paper for printers; (4) software and any associated instructional materials; and (5) miscellaneous costs, such as insurance, maintenance, and energy.

Technology is widely believed to make instruction more efficient and hence more cost-effective. In part, this belief is probably an extrapolation from observed effects of technology on productivity in the workplace. There is empirical support for the position as well. A widely cited study by the Institute for Defense Analyses compared the cost of computer-based instruction to that of stand-up training per unit of achievement in military training programs and found that CAI was, on average, 30 percent less expensive (Fletcher & Orlansky 1986). These cost-savings stemmed from faster learning, with associated reductions in personnel and travel costs.

Levin (1989) analyzed cost and effectiveness data for eight mathematics and reading CAI programs implemented in the 1980s. To achieve a given increment in student test scores, CAI proved more cost-effective than reducing class size, extending the length of the school day, or using adult tutors, but considerably less so than peer tutoring. Levin noted that both effectiveness and costs varied markedly from site to site, even though the CAI under study was fairly structured, standardized drill and practice. He concluded that results depend heavily on how the CAI is implemented at the particular site, and that CAI could be much more cost effective if it were not underutilized.

Delineating all cost elements and placing a value on them can help dispel misconceptions about the relative price of different instructional technologies. For instance, it is widely argued that because the cost of computers is dropping so rapidly, current cost comparisons that favor conventional approaches will soon be totally irrelevant. Levin (1989) points out that computer hardware and peripheral costs are too small a proportion of the total cost of CAI implementations for this to be true. Even if all hardware costs were reduced to zero, the total cost of the average intervention studied by Levin (i.e., fairly straightforward drill-and-practice CAI programs) would be reduced by only 11 percent.

Cost comparisons between distance-learning and face-to-face training within the corporate and military training sectors nearly always favor the former (Moore 1989). These findings should not be extrapolated to K-12 education without careful examination. The primary reason for the cost advantage of these technologies in corporate and military training is the large savings in travel expenses and travel time for personnel who must be trained (expense categories with less relevance for K-12 education). A national survey on the cost-effectiveness of distance-learning in schools found that the cost per student was lower with distance-learning than with a live teacher in only 15 of 34 classes (Ellertson, Wydra & Jolley 1987). Thus, distance-learning is not necessarily more cost-effective in a school setting (but it may be the only viable alternative if qualified instructors are not available locally).

A problem with these cost-effectiveness studies is that they depend on the kind of comparative study described above for their index of program efficacy. The measures of effectiveness used in the primary studies may capture the objectives of some programs better than others. For example, Slavin (1991) reanalyzed data from evaluations of the *Writing to Read* program and concluded that other kindergarten reading programs, costing on the order of 1 percent of the price of *Writing to Read*, are equally effective. However, Slavin used scores on standardized tests of reading achievement as the measure of effectiveness. The test items were more like the contents of the competing reading programs than the *Writing to Read* activities. Slavin dismisses effects on expressive writing skills (which would be similar to *Writing to Read* activities but not to most of the competing programs) as irrelevant to the decision to adopt such a program. The measures used to estimate effect size need to be scrutinized; policymakers may or may not share the analyst's viewpoint concerning the outcomes that are relevant in comparing program efficacy.

More fundamentally, many in the education reform movement object to the cost-benefit studies, because they perpetuate the view that the reason for using technology is to do the same things faster. Those who regard technology as a tool for education reform—who see it as contributing to the adoption of a higher set of expectations for students, to more emphasis on complex tasks and collaborative learning, to a change in the roles of students and teachers—contend that an analysis showing that computers can teach lower-level skills faster than can worksheets simply misses the point.

Chapter VI
Implementation Issues

Why Reforms Fail

In and of themselves, technologies are essentially neutral with respect to instructional principles. A given technology can be used to support almost any instructional philosophy. Thus, computers can be (and have been) used as an "electronic page turner" for didactic text, with students doing nothing more than pushing the Return key to see the next segment. The same computer can become the medium for purely exploratory approaches, as students browse through hypermedia stacks, or can be used by the student as a tool for displaying and reflecting on a complex set of data. Putting computers or a satellite link or telefacsimile machines into schools does not necessarily do anything to change the basic instructional philosophy, curricular content, or student–teacher roles. The fact that these technologies *can* be used to deliver instruction that stresses thinking, solving complex problems, and interdisciplinary work does not mean that they *will* be.

Several critics argue that today's instructional technologies are simply the latest in a long line of innovations that have been touted as the instrument for transforming schools. What happens instead is that the technology is either adapted to traditional school structures and teaching styles, if it is sufficiently flexible, or discarded if it cannot be so adapted (Cohen 1988; Cuban 1986). Cohen contends that the dominant use of distance-learning is wider dissemination of a traditional mode of teaching: the lecture. Similarly, microcomputers provide an on-line version of the drill-and-practice "seatwork" that has long been a staple of the elementary school classroom. Piele (1989) asserts that although microcomputers have found their way into schools in large numbers, they have failed to transform schools because they are typically set off in a computer "lab," usually supervised by someone other than the classroom teacher. Thus, most teachers can and do "ignore them altogether" (p. 95). Cohen concludes that uses of instructional technology that break the mold of conventional instruction are most likely to be adopted "at the margins," that is, in advanced placement courses, special education, or vocational training. The central instructional program remains much as it was 50 years ago, untouched by the technological revolution going on around it.

Why hasn't technology made a real difference in the teaching and learning that go on in more schools? The greatest part of the explanation resides in the imperviousness of the education system to any kind of *— incapable of being penetrated* fundamental change; the barriers that are specific to technology-based changes are very real, but a lesser impediment. As Sheingold (1991b) puts it:

It is now well understood that the challenge of integrating technology into schools and classrooms is much more human than it is technological. What's more, it is not fundamentally about helping people to operate machines. Rather, it is about helping people, primarily teachers, integrate these technologies into their teaching as tools of a profession that is being redefined through the incorporation process. (p. 1)

Smith and O'Day (1990) have argued that current calls for education reform seek a fundamental change in both the content and pedagogy of the classroom. This reform agenda confronts a fragmented, complicated system of education decision-making that involves many different agencies and levels within agencies and provides few incentives for lasting change. While various agents push one new approach or the other, teachers "close their classroom doors and teach as they were taught" (p. 238). The dominant curricula and commercially produced materials, stressing breadth of "coverage" over analytic problem solving, the high-stakes assessment system consisting predominantly of multiple-choice tests stressing basic skills or unconnected facts, and the training of teachers all support conventional schooling.

Nevertheless, technology can be used in ways that support reform goals for education, as illustrated in many of the projects described here in earlier chapters. When technology is used in these ways, it exerts pressure on the system for change. Salomon (1991) describes how this happened in an eighth-grade class studying the U.S. Constitution. The research team introduced the notion that this topic could be approached by having students set up an electronic database on the Constitution. According to Salomon, the database became a "Trojan horse" bringing with it radical changes in everything else about the class (p. 12). Students split into teams representing the different factions at the time the Constitution was drafted. The teams prepared for a reenactment of the Constitutional Convention at which each faction argued for wording changes that would benefit their own group. A new role emerged for the teacher, who "hovered around, directing, guiding, suggesting, and advising, more like an orchestra conductor than a music composer" (p. 12).

Newman (1990a) describes how technology can begin to soften the rigid boundaries between traditional class periods, subject areas, and years of school. Students involved in the Earth Lab project were able to use the workspace provided on the network to continue working on assignments after shifting physical locations, simply logging onto the system from a different computer. Small work groups that were set up and assigned a computer workspace in science classes started to be used by teachers in other courses. Students started using weather data that had been collected by the class the previous year. Thus, the usually rigid boundaries between subject areas, physical locations, and school year were being chipped away as new social structures and work habits emerged.

Sheingold and Hadley (1990) conducted a survey of teachers noted for incorporating technology into their practice. These teachers reported that they are able to present more complex material, that students proceed more independently, and that their role as teachers has shifted from providing information to coaching. In addition, computer software can affect teachers' practice by providing them with models for the kinds of complex, interdisciplinary tasks they could be teaching (Sheingold 1990). The new math instructional programs described in Chapter II had their most lasting impact on the teachers, who internalized the content presented on the videos and began teaching it themselves.

Lessons from Implementation Studies

An increasing number of studies of technology use in schools have focused on the implementation process and provide a basis for preliminary recommendations regarding the use of technology to support education reform.

Need to Start With Instructional Goals

Many of the horror stories concerning television sets stacked in school closets and computers still in their boxes reflect the unfortunate situation where technologies are purchased for their own sake rather than as a means to an instructional goal. Those who market technologies recognize this tendency, as indicated by two software marketers interviewed by Levin and Meister (1985):

> Schools find it hard to know where they're going with computers. No one knows. Schools are really just trying to keep up.

> Despite all the advice that says to look at the courseware first, schools never look at software first. [They acquire computers and then search for software.] They're so quick to spend money, they end up doing it haphazardly. (p. 24)

We have argued that technologies per se do not embody a particular set of curricular or pedagogical goals. The writing of Cuban (1986), Cohen (1988), and others suggests that unless the school staff start out with an instructional goal, technology is most likely to be used to reinforce the status quo. Piele (1989) argues that this is exactly what happened with microcomputers in most schools, where they became a drain on resources and just added to the burdens of teachers who already were trying to do too much.

Most teachers will find little incentive to tackle the technical and scheduling problems associated with technology, unless they have a clear vision of how the technology can improve teaching and learning. Calfee (1991) argues that education reform requires the involvement not just of the classroom but of the school as a whole. If students are to experience a new kind of education that places real value on extended intellectual effort and problem solving, this kind of thinking needs to be encouraged not just in one unit or one class or even in one year but throughout the student's school experience. This requires a school's teachers to come together and to work with administrators to develop a unifying set of goals. Although principles may be embodied somewhat differently in different classrooms, adherence to a consistent set of principles can unify the school. Given reformers' goals such as those we outlined in the introduction (i.e., use of authentic, challenging multidisciplinary tasks; promotion of active learning and collaborative work; and so on), schools will find that there is much they can start doing to prepare students for this kind of work without technology—for example, working on collaborative research projects with traditional paper-based tools. Schools participating in California's Model Technology Schools program found that a common set of instructional goals to work on was important in maintaining project identity and momentum when they encountered the inevitable delays in the delivery of hardware and software (M. Stearns et al. 1991). Such activities prepare students and teachers for their new roles in subsequent technology-enhanced projects. Moreover, they start moving the school toward education reform now, without waiting for the approvals, funding, delivery, and training that precede the use of new technology.

Importance of Connections to Curricular Goals and Frameworks

Often, technology does not get used because the available software is simply irrelevant to the teacher's curricular goals. The decentralization of American education and the resulting diversification of curriculum content have made it uneconomical for the developers of instructional courseware to develop products to match every curriculum. Most of the more sophisticated, inventive pieces of instructional software deal with only a narrow slice of curriculum (Levin & Meister 1985) or with material that is fairly trivial in and of itself (Rockman 1991). At the same time, teachers report intense pressure to "cover" an unrealistically large amount of required material. Teachers see instructional software that does not match their curriculum as a distraction, fine for enrichment for students proceeding rapidly and for basic skills remediation for slower students, but not central to their basic curricular goals.

This problem can be attacked on two fronts. First, teachers and schools can be involved in efforts to modify the curriculum and to develop a more realistic set of curriculum goals. The requirement to "cover" too many topics in a given time period has led to superficial treatment, with students learning the names but little else for many of the concepts they are studying. Many reform efforts are pointing toward greater depth in covering fewer topics and toward more local-school involvement in determining what those topics should be. This trend will make it easier to incorporate technology in teaching and learning the key concepts and skills that are to be emphasized in the new curriculum. At the same time, as Wiske, Niguidula, and Shepard (1988) report, teachers who are able to participate in renegotiating curriculum and assessment requirements are more likely to consider using computers in ways that support education reform.

A second way to approach the problem is by encouraging the development of software materials that are compatible with curricular goals. As described in Chapter IV, technology can provide tools for teachers to use in creating their own materials. Evaluators have noted, however, the great investment in time and effort that such projects require. Often, teachers prefer to have the opportunity to do some tailoring of materials for their own purposes, without having to do the basic development (Wiske, Zodhiates, Wilson et al. 1988, and the *Catlab* example in Chapter IV).

The state of California recognized the importance of the match between technology-based materials and the existing curriculum and has been a leader in addressing the issue. The state established funds to set up partnerships between developers and the California Department of Education. The state provides seed money for the development of technology-based materials geared to state curriculum frameworks; developers coinvest with substantial matching funds; California schools get discounts on the resulting materials, and the state receives royalties based on the materials' out-of-state sales (O'Connor 1991). One of the early products of this arrangement, *GTV, The American Experience*, developed by the National Geographic Society, Apple Computer, and LucasFilm, won awards for quality and earned back the developers' investment within the first 6 months. A current project, *Science 2000*, is aligned with California's science framework for seventh graders and is intended to be a full, exemplary science curriculum taught using computer software, video- and audiotapes, videodisc, hands-on materials, text, and telecommunications.

Compatibility With Assessment System

Concern over the quality of education and the resolve to hold schools accountable for student learning have made assessment a "high-stakes" activity. Districts and schools are rewarded and punished on the basis of the average test scores of their students. In striving for comparability across sites and for cost-effectiveness, the standardized tests that are used for these evaluations consist almost entirely of multiple-choice questions covering many discrete topics. Basic skills are stressed. To avoid favoring one curriculum topic over the other, test developers measure reading comprehension using material that is likely to be new to everyone. Thus, particular knowledge that may have been learned, the ability to regulate one's own sustained intellectual inquiry, and advanced skills generally go untested. The education system may unwittingly subvert efforts to teach more advanced skills by judging districts, schools, principals, and teachers on the basis of their students' performance on basic-skills tests. The surest way to raise those test scores is to teach to the tests; time spent with technology-enhanced instruction aimed at very different learning outcomes becomes a "distraction."

The potential for high-stakes testing of content that is not the goal of an innovation to kill off a project was demonstrated at the Belridge School in McKittrick, California. Funded by tax revenues from neighboring oil fields, this small K-8 school district purchased computers for school and home use for every student and teacher in the school. Laser disc players, television production equipment, and large amounts of software were purchased. The project stressed having students collaborate on meaningful tasks that would challenge them to think. Student work included producing their own television news shows and setting up and administering a computer-based presidential election. Two years later, when scores on the Iowa Test of Basic Skills for the first year of the technology implementation were released, parents were shocked to see that their students scored no better than before and slightly below the national median. Failing to consider the difference in focus between the technology-based projects and the standardized test and the immaturity of the implementation at the time the students were tested, parents picketed the school and elected a new school board with the mandate to find a new "back to basics" principal. Computers were removed from student desks and pushed to the rear of the classroom or sold (Schulz 1992).

Thus, it is wise for innovators to confront the assessment issue as early as possible. Although district and state testing policies may be beyond local control, the school or classroom can at least take steps to collect additional assessment data that are more compatible with the goals of their innovation. Unfortunately, we lack good standardized measures of many advanced thinking skills, but a school can at least choose among the more appropriate subtests from standardized test batteries (e.g., reading comprehension as opposed to word attack skills, math problem solving as opposed to numerical operations) and can supplement these measures with writing samples, portfolios, and other concrete evidence of student achievement.

Teachers and Technology Need to Work Together

Many of the early technology enthusiasts dreamed of a "teacher-proof" system embodying sound principles of teaching and learning and engaging students directly without the interference of a teacher whose knowledge base might be incomplete or whose pedagogy might be faulty. Studies of classroom implementations of technology have demonstrated that this goal was not only unrealistic but wrongheaded. Teachers can subvert practically any kind of instructional material to their own goals and ways of teaching (Cuban 1986). At the same time, even the best software programs will be inadequate for many students under many circumstances. Zorfass (1991) describes the abysmal failure of the *Carmen Sandiego* program with a class of inner-city students who were not fluent in English and knew little about geography, American culture, or how to use reference materials. Lacking the needed background, they could not engage in the kind of problem solving the game was designed to evoke. Only when the teacher developed an instructional program around the software, having students work in small groups rather than individually and teaching skills and knowledge needed to play the game, were students able to profit from it.

Delclos and Kulewicz (1986) studied sixth-grade children's use of *Rocky's Boots*, a highly regarded piece of software for teaching problem-solving skills. Without help from a teacher, most of the children in the study could solve fewer than half of the 39 problems in the program. The researchers described students as "hitting a plateau" in their independent work. When teachers intervened, providing instruction on problem-solving strategies within the context of the specific problems in the programs, students were able to go far beyond their initial level of independent problem solving. Thus, experience suggests that the most successful projects will be those in which the intervention incorporates both teacher activities and technology into a broader learning activity.

Requirement for Ongoing Pedagogical and Technological Support

Wiske et al. (1988) interviewed 76 teachers concerning their experiences with integrating computers into their classrooms. The teachers were nearly unanimous in concluding that initially the use of computers made teaching more difficult. They not only had to plan how technology could be incorporated into their lessons but also had to work through the logistical problems of deciding which students would use the computers at what times. Hardware and software problems are common in the early stages of an implementation. Evaluations of the Model Technology Schools in California (M. Stearns et al. 1991) documented similar problems and found that the presence of on-site assistance with the technology is critical for success. Districts found that moving technical assistance personnel from a central site out into the schools during the implementation process was important in making curricular and instructional improvements happen.

The need to train teachers when introducing technology was illustrated also in the experience of the San Francisco schools with multimedia systems. Seventeen systems were installed in 1989 along with social studies and history software developed by the National Geographic Society. Most of the machines were idle at the end of that school year, however. Only after teachers were given training in how to work the multimedia content into their lesson plans did teachers start using the technology available to them (Yoder 1991).

Even if the technology and its content did not pose challenges to teachers, the new curricula and teaching strategies associated with education reform would. Introducing complex, multidisciplinary projects and a strong element of student control means opening the door for students to explore content areas that are unknown to the teacher. Acting as a coach for small groups of students working cooperatively requires diagnostic and management skills that are not called on when teaching is equated with lecturing. Smith and O'Day (1990) point out that pre-service education for teachers does not equip them for these roles. Teachers need support for deepening their knowledge of content areas and for learning new teaching skills. Both outside advisors and fellow teachers trying to implement the same or similar innovations can serve this function effectively.

Role of Community Involvement

The push toward use of technology in the classroom often comes from outside the school. Parents and business representatives, seeing how technology has transformed the workplace and concerned for the economic survival of their children and their community, press schools to capitalize on the presumed efficiency and power of using technology. However, such calls for the infusion of technology into schools are not usually accompanied by any clear ideas concerning just what should be taught using technology or how it should be taught. The chances for success are increased when parents and the community buy into the instructional goals of the reform and understand the implications in terms of costs, other forgone activities, and likely effects on test scores.

The effective schools literature showing the value of parent and community involvement (Epstein 1984; Herman & Yeh 1983) implies that these groups should be made participants in the process of technology-supported education reform. Partnership means sharing in developing the instructional goals of the reform and taking responsibility for helping to support them. This requires much more than unfocused enthusiasm concerning computers or videoconferencing.

Obtaining community understanding and support will not always be easy. Education reform goals, as we have described them here, are based on a particular (constructivist) view of learning. This view is in direct contention with conventional notions of knowledge as a set of facts and teaching as the telling of facts. Cohen (1988) points out the prevalence of the conventional view:

> Contrary to most reformers' beliefs, these [conventional] views elicit profound attachment from many children and adults.... The conceptions and practices that reformers wish to replace are not simply obsolete, boring, and stupid impositions.... Traditional approaches to instruction contain coherent and defensible views of knowledge, teaching, and learning.... One part of this scholastic inheritance is the widely shared conviction that valid academic knowledge consists of facts. Facts are found in books and teachers' lectures. Efforts to suggest that there is more to academic knowledge than facts—that it consists of ideas about facts, or that facts have no meaningful status unless embedded in ideas about them, or that students are authors of ideas and therefore creators of academic knowledge—violate this view. For if knowledge does not consist of facts, well established and stored in authoritative locations, how can it be trusted? Anyone can make up ideas. If knowledge is composed or constructed—which is to say, made up—by little children, or even by schoolteachers, how seriously can it be taken? (pp. 256-257)

The experiences of the Belridge School described above provide a dramatic demonstration of the risks involved when the community does not fully understand or embrace the instructional goals of an innovation. A misunderstanding of the project's intentions and likely outcomes led to a community backlash that not only killed the school project but produced technology-bashing headlines ("The revolution that fizzled") in a national news magazine (Elmer-Dewitt 1991) as well.

The Role of Business

An important player in the introduction of technology into school reform is corporate America. In 1989, the U.S. Department of Education estimated that there were over 140,000 business-school partnerships in the United States. Given the importance of technology in the workplace and business' concern with having a technically literate future workforce, many of the corporations have sought to foster the introduction of technology into the schools they support. Not surprisingly, computer equipment manufacturers are in the forefront. Both Apple and IBM are estimated to have provided over $50 million in computers and related equipment to schools during the 1980s (Perry 1990). AT&T's involvement has included the donation of a $250,000 fiberoptics-based wideband switching system to a Los Angeles high school. Scores of other companies have donated equipment or provided support for technology use by making technically qualified company staff available to school students or personnel.

Although donations of equipment and technical support can be vital in a time of tight school budgets, we have argued that technology per se does not make school reform happen. An increasing number of corporations have come to share this view and are becoming involved in longer-term partnerships, attempting to implement one or more pieces of the reform agenda. For example, the Panasonic Foundation has funded school districts for major school-restructuring experiments. These partnerships last from 5 to 10 years, during which Panasonic provides technical assistance and consultants to help the school redesign itself (Rigden 1991). In an ongoing project funded by Panasonic, the Center for Children and Technology at Bank Street College was invited to work with schools to study how laptop computers could be used to support student and teacher learning. In one eighth-grade class that is part of a restructured "school within a school," all students have laptops plus software to enable them to compose, analyze data, and prepare graphs. These tools are being used within a research-based curriculum that calls on students to both analyze data and write about a variety of science topics. An Apple Computer project, the Christopher Columbus Consortium, pairs school districts and universities to explore ways in which technology can be used to improve instruction. IBM gives grants to schools of education for the purpose of developing programs to prepare new teachers for the technology-laden classroom of the future. Another Apple program, the Apple Classrooms of Tomorrow (ACOT), includes not only the infusion of large amounts of technology but also technical support in using technology in ways that support student-centered classrooms.

Models for the Growth of Education Reform

How can education reform and technology's positive role in that reform proceed? Critics such as Cohen (1988) and Cuban (1986) provide a sobering perspective on the prospects for real change. It won't just happen; certainly the purchase of computers or videodisc players or satellite links, even in much larger quantities than we see today, won't automatically bring about the transformation in student learning activities that reformers envision.

State-Initiated, Top-Down Reform

Although the United States still has the most decentralized education system in the industrialized world, many states are taking a more and more active role, taking on curriculum and programmatic decisions that were formerly district and school prerogatives. California's curriculum frameworks set specific learning goals in seven content areas and suggest instructional approaches. California has also developed a textbook adoption policy that stresses compatibility with the advanced-skills emphasis in its curriculum frameworks. Florida is requiring all schools to develop plans to attain specific state-mandated outcomes. Texas is setting standards for student and teacher workstations and is phasing in standards for access time per week.

The justification for state planning and activity is particularly strong if technology is considered an integral part of reform, because states can garner both technical resources and leverage in equipment and software purchases that would be hard for a school to duplicate.

Previous research on top-down educational innovations (e.g., Berman & McLaughlin 1978) does not engender confidence concerning the efficacy of purely top-down approaches, however. When required to adopt an innovation, districts and schools have a tendency to take on its superficial features without really incorporating its substance. In a recent study of the academic instruction received by disadvantaged students, SRI found that many teachers reverted to more accustomed modes of conventional instruction despite state mandates for new curricula and more innovative materials (Knapp et al. 1992).

The problems with mandated use of technology were illustrated in a middle school studied by Zorfass et al. (1989). When the district decided that all eighth-grade mathematics teachers had to provide LOGO instruction once a week for 10 weeks, many teachers felt the program was forced on them. Uncomfortable with computers in general and LOGO in particular, they saw no fit between LOGO and what they were trying to teach. Some thought it belonged in sophomore geometry, some in art; others saw no reason for it whatsoever. Feeling that they had too little time to cover the required standard curriculum anyway, they were acutely aware of the time the LOGO program took away from their regular program. They went through the motions of teaching LOGO, but only a few teachers tried to find interesting ways to teach it or to connect it to the rest of their curriculum.

Classroom-Initiated, Bottom-Up Reform

The opposite of the state-initiated top-down model is a completely grass-roots effort. Under this model, an individual school or even a classroom decides to redesign itself. This model is most in keeping with the reform goal of site-based management and has important advantages in that teachers will better understand and implement an innovation that they themselves develop.

Although laboring within systems that may be more or less hostile to radical change, schools and classrooms are implementing innovative programs. Some of the kinds of project-based, inquiry-oriented work that individual sites are doing with the help of technology are described in preceding chapters. Most of these programs started with one or two individuals who were personally committed to transforming their classrooms with technology.

These local activities deserve to be commended, but we must be concerned that they will remain scattered and hit-or-miss. Some exceptionally dedicated teachers will put in the time and energy to conceive and implement such programs, at least for a while. Their students will benefit from their work and gain a new confidence in their ability to learn using technology. Most students will never receive this kind of instruction, however, if there is no systemic support for it. Although there are anecdotes of innovative methods and materials spreading from one or two classrooms to others within a school, there are also stories of schools dividing themselves into the "project teachers and students" and the "other teachers and students," with the attendant atmosphere of divisiveness. Innovations have a fragile existence, particularly when they are not consistent with a state or district curriculum and accountability measures. Without institutional support, innovations die off when their champion leaves or becomes discouraged. In their study of technology implementation in middle schools, Morocco et al. (1989) found that technology applications were more likely to be sustained when they were considered a school-based effort and cut across multiple classrooms and content domains.

In addition to the greater staying power of innovations supported by the broader educational system, there are significant economic and political arguments for broader-based reform efforts. Initiatives involving telecommunications technologies require larger-scale involvement by their very nature. Economies of purchasing and planning technology acquisitions argue for the involvement of state or regional-level agencies (Council of Chief State School Officers 1991). States also have an important role in guaranteeing equality of access. Student homes vary dramatically in the amount of technology available, and without state action, differences among schools serving advantaged and disadvantaged students are likely to reinforce such inequalities.

Mixed Initiatives

The discussion of the two models above suggests the need for a third, hybrid model of reform implementation. In a hybrid model, the state can provide a structure within which local initiatives receive funding and become part of a dissemination network. Here, the state takes the lead in setting an agenda for reform but recognizes the importance of local initiative and of letting classrooms and teachers "invent themselves." Under this model, the state's role is to create the structure for reform but not the detailed content. Funding, technical assistance, and waivers from regulations can be used to support local reform. In the technology area, model schools programs, support for inservice training, funding for local development of technology-based materials, and development of a telecommunications infrastructure are some of the steps states are taking.

While providing leadership and support, the state leaves the essential design and implementation issues to local control. California and Washington have funded local school restructuring projects. These states and others have provided support for model technology schools. State funding competitions for technology-enhanced reform programs can serve as a catalyst for local schools and districts to take action. Such competitions often stimulate the formation of local working groups; partnerships with business, the community, and universities; and the generation and elaboration of ideas for improving teaching and learning. Often, even schools and districts that fail to obtain state funding go ahead and implement aspects of the projects they have designed.

There is much more to learn about how this mixed-initiative model gets played out and how state technology reform initiatives can ultimately affect student learning in the classroom. It seems clear, however, that both higher levels of the education system and local schools and teachers will have to be players if we are to really reform the education received by all our students.

References

Agency for Instructional Technology. (1987). *A survey of the use of technology with students at risk of school failure.* Bloomington, IN: Author.

Anderson, J. R., Boyle, C. F., & Yost, G. (1985). The geometry tutor. *Proceedings of the 9th International Joint Conference on Artificial Intelligence* (pp. 1-7), Los Angeles.

Bangert-Drowns, R. L., Kulik, J. A., & Kulik, C. C. (1985). Effectiveness of computer-based education in secondary schools. *Journal of Computer-Based Instruction, 12*(3), 59-68.

Barron, B., & Rieser, J. (1992). *Collaborative problem solving: Effects on initial performance, mastery, and transfer for students of three achievement levels.* Paper presented at the annual meeting of the American Educational Research Association, San Francisco.

Becker, H. J. (1983). *School uses of microcomputers: Reports from a national survey.* Baltimore, MD: Center for Social Organization of Schools, Johns Hopkins University.

Becker, H. J. (1985). How schools use microcomputers: Results from a national survey. In M. Chen & W. Paisley (Eds.), *Children and microcomputers: Research on the newest medium* (pp. 87-107). Beverly Hills, CA: Sage.

Becker, H. J. (1990, April). *Computer use in United States schools: 1989. An initial report of U.S. participation in the I.E.A. Computers in Education Survey.* Paper presented at the annual meeting of the American Educational Research Association, Boston.

Becker, H. J., & Sterling, C. W. (1987). Equity in school computer use: National data and neglected considerations. *Journal of Educational Computing Research, 3*(3), 289-311.

Bennett, D. A., & King, D. T. (1991, May). The Saturn School of Tomorrow. *Educational Leadership,* pp. 41-44.

Berger, S. (1989). Toward "real science": The TERC Star Schools project. *Hands On!, 12*(2), 1, 12-13.

Berman, P., & McLaughlin, M. (1978). *Federal programs supporting educational change.* V*ol. VIII* of *Implementing and sustaining innovations.* Santa Monica, CA: Rand.

Bialo, E., & Sivin, J. (1990). *Report on the effectiveness of microcomputers in schools.* Washington, DC: Software Publishers Association.

Borg, K. (1985). *The effects on children's writing of adding speech synthesis to a word processor.* Unpublished doctoral dissertation, University of Wisconsin.

Bosco, J. (1986, May). An analysis of evaluations of interactive video. *Educational Technology*, pp. 7-17.

Bransford, J. D., Goin, L. I., Hasselbring, T. S., Kinzer, C. Z., Sherwood, R. D., & Williams, S. M. (1988). Learning with technology: Theoretical and empirical perspectives. *Peabody Journal of Education, 64*(1), 5-26.

Bransford, J. D., Sherwood, R. S., Hasselbring, T. S., Kinzer, C. K., & Williams, S. M. (1989). Anchored instruction: Why we need it and how technology can help. In D. Nix & R. Spiro (Eds.), *Advances in computer-video technology.* Hillsdale, NJ: Erlbaum.

Bryant, J., Alexander, A. F., & Brown, D. (1983). Learning from educational television programs. In M.J.A. Howe (Ed.), *Learning from television: Psychological and educational research.* Orlando, FL: Academic Press.

Brasell, H. (1987). The effect of real-time laboratory graphing on learning graphic representations of distance and velocity. *Journal of Research in Science Teaching, 24*(4), 385-395.

Bremer, J. (1991, September). Saturn: A school of the future. *The World & I*, pp. 239-247.

Brophy, J. (1987, October). Synthesis of research on strategies for motivating students to learn. *Educational Leadership*, pp. 40-48.

Brown, A. L. (1992). Design experiments: Theoretical and methodological challenges in creating complex interventions in classroom settings. *Journal of the Learning Sciences, 2*(2), 141-178.

Brown, A. L., Ash, D., Rutherford, M., Nakagawa, K., Gordon, A., & Campione, J. C. (In press). Distributed expertise in the classroom. To appear in G. Salomon (Ed.), *Distributed cognitions.* New York: Cambridge University Press.

Brown, J. S., & Burton, R. R. (1978). Diagnostic models for procedural bugs in basic mathematical skills. *Cognitive Science, 2*, 155-192.

Brown, J. S., Collins, A., & Duguid, P. (1989). Situated cognition and the culture of learning. *Educational Researcher, 18*(1), 32-42.

Bryson, M., & Scardamalia, M. (1991). Teaching writing to students at risk for academic failure. In B. Means, C. Chelemer, & M. S. Knapp (Eds.), *Teaching advanced skills to at-risk students: Views from research and practice.* San Francisco: Jossey-Bass.

Calfee, R. (1991). What schools can do to improve literacy instruction. In B. Means, C. Chelemer, & M. S. Knapp (Eds.), *Teaching advanced skills to at-risk students: Views from research and practice.* San Francisco: Jossey-Bass.

Campione, J. C., Brown, A. L., & Jay, M. (1992). Computers in a community of learners. In E. DeCorte & M. Linn (Eds.), *Computer-based learning environments and problem solving.* New York: Springer-Verlag.

Center for Technology in Education. (1991, March). Design experiments: A new kind of research. *Technology and Learning,* pp. 28-29.

Chen, M. (1991). *Educational video: What works?* (A position paper for the Hughes Public Education Project). San Francisco: KQED Television.

Clark, R. E. (1985). Evidence for confounding in computer-based instruction studies: Analyzing the meta-analyses. *Educational Communication and Technology Journal, 33*(4), 249-262.

Coburn, P., Kelman, P., Roberts, N., Snyder, T.F.F., Watt, D. H., & Weiner, C. (1982). *Practical guide to computers in education.* Reading, MA: Addison-Wesley.

Cognition and Technology Group at Vanderbilt. (1990). Anchored instruction and its relationship to situated cognition. *Educational Researcher, 19*(6), 2-10.

Cognition and Technology Group at Vanderbilt. (1991). Technology and the design of generative learning environments. *Educational Technology Journal, 31*(5), 34-40.

Cohen, D. K. (1988). Educational technology and school organization. In R. S. Nickerson & P. P. Zodhiates (Eds.), *Technology in education: Looking toward 2020* (pp. 231-264). Hillsdale, NJ: Erlbaum.

Collins, A. (1990). The role of computer technology in restructuring schools. In K. Sheingold & M. S. Tucker (Eds.), *Restructuring for learning with technology.* New York: Center for Technology in Education, Bank Street College of Education; and Rochester, NY: National Center on Education and the Economy.

Collins, A., Brown, J. S., & Newman, S. E. (1989). Cognitive apprenticeship: Teaching the craft of reading, writing, and mathematics. In L. B. Resnick (Ed.), *Knowing, learning, and instruction: Essays in honor of Robert Glaser* (pp. 453-494). Hillsdale, NJ: Erlbaum.

Collins, A., Hawkins, J., & Carver, S. M. (1991). A cognitive apprenticeship for disadvantaged students. In B. Means, C. Chelemer, & M. S. Knapp (Eds.), *Teaching advanced skills to at-risk students: views from research and practice*. San Francisco: Jossey-Bass.

Collins, A., Hawkins, J., & Fredriksen, J. R. (1991). *Three different views of students: The role of technology in assessing student performance* (Technical Report No. 12). New York: Bank Street College of Education.

Comer, J. P. (1988). Educating poor minority children. *Scientific American, 259*(5), 42-48.

Council of Chief State School Officers. (1991, November 11). *Improving student performance through learning technologies*. Policy statement.

Cuban, L. (1986). *Teachers and machines: The classroom use of technology since 1920*. New York: Teachers College Press.

Daiute, C. (1986). Physical and cognitive factors in revising: Insights from studies with computers. *Research in the Teaching of English, 20*, 141-159.

David, J. L. (1989). *Restructuring in progress: Lessons from pioneering districts*. Washington, DC: National Governors' Association, Center for Policy Research.

David, J. L., & Shields, P. M. (1991). *From effective schools to restructuring: A literature review*. Menlo Park, CA: SRI International.

Delclos, V. R., & Kulewicz, S. J. (1986). Improving computer-based problem solving training: The role of the teacher as mediator. *Computers and Human Behavior, 2*, 135-146.

DeVillar, R. A., & Faltis, C. J. (1991). *Computers and cultural diversity: Restructuring for school success*. Albany, NY: State University of New York Press.

Dickinson, D. (1986). Cooperation, collaboration, and a computer: Integrating a computer into a first-second grade writing program. *Research in the Teaching of English, 20*, 357-378.

Douglas, S. G., & Bransford, L. A. (1991). Advanced technologies: Innovations and applications for distance learning. In A. D. Sheekey (Ed.), *Education Policy and Telecommunications Technologies*. Washington, DC: Office of Educational Research and Improvement.

Driscoll, M., & Kelemanik, G. (1991, December). *Electronic communication and community building*. Paper presented at Telecommunication as a Tool for Educational Reform: Implementing the NCTM Standards, The Aspen Institute.

Duffy, T. M., & Knuth, R. A. (1989, July). *Hypermedia and instruction: Where is the match?* Paper presented at the NATO Conference on Designing Hypertext for Learning, Tubingen, West Germany. To appear in D. Jonassen & H. Mandl (Eds.), *Designing hypermedia for learning*. Heidelberg, West Germany: Springer-Verlag.

Dwyer, D. C., Ringstaff, C., & Sandholtz, J. (1990). *The evolution of teachers' instructional beliefs and practices in high-access-to-technology classrooms*. Paper presented at the annual meeting of the American Educational Research Association, Boston.

Ellertson, K. K., Wydra, D., & Jolley, H. (1987). *Report on distance learning: A national effectiveness survey*. Mansfield, PA: Mansfield University and the Pennsylvania Department of Education.

Elmer-Dewitt, P. (1991, May 20). The revolution that fizzled: Computers have not lived up to their promise to transform America's struggling schools, but it's not too late to redeem the failure. *Time*, p. 48.

Epstein, J. (1984). School policy and parent involvement. *Educational Horizons, 62,* 70-72.

FCCSET Committee on Education and Human Resources. (1991). *By the year 2000: First in the world*. Washington, DC: Office of Science and Technology Policy, Federal Coordinating Council for Science, Engineering, and Technology.

Fletcher, J. D. (1990). *Effectiveness and cost of interactive videodisc instruction in defense training and education*. Alexandria, VA: Institute for Defense Analyses.

Fletcher, J. D. & Orlansky, J. (1986). *Cost effectiveness of CBI in defense training*. Paper presented at the annual meeting of the American Educational Research Association, San Francisco.

Fullan, M. G. (1990). Staff development, innovation, and institutional development. In B. Joyce (Ed.), *Changing school culture through staff development (1990 Yearbook of the Association for Supervision and Curriculum Development, pp. 3-25)*. Alexandria, VA: Association for Supervision and Curriculum Development.

Gillingham, M.G. (1991). In search of a dynabook. *The Computing Teacher, 19* (2), 9-14.

Gragg, C. I. (1940). Because wisdom can't be told. *Harvard Alumni Bulletin*, pp. 78-84.

Griffin, P., & Cole, M. (1987). New technologies, basic skills, and the underside of education: What's to be done? In J. A. Langer (Ed.), *Language, literacy, and culture: Issues of society and schooling* (pp. 199-231). Norwood, NJ: Ablex.

Hall, E. R., Esty, E. T., & Fisch, S. M. (1990). Television and children's problem-solving behavior: A synopsis of an evaluation of the effects of *Square One TV*. *Journal of Mathematical Behavior*, *9*, 161-174.

Harasim, L. M. (1990). Online education: An environment for collaboration and intellectual amplification. In L. M. Harasim (Ed.), *Online education: Perspectives on a new environment* (pp. 39-64). New York: Praeger.

Hasselbring, T., Goin, L., Zhou, L., Alcantara, P., & Musil, S. (1992, January). *Cognitive challenges and pedagogical opportunities of integrated media systems.* Presentation at International Conference, Technology and Media (TAM), Division of the Council for Exceptional Children, Albuquerque.

Hawkins, J., & Sheingold, K. (1985). The beginning of a story: Computers and the organization of learning in classrooms. In *Microcomputers and education: 85th yearbook of the National Society for the Study of Education.* Chicago: University of Chicago Press.

Heap, J. L. (1986, April). *Collaborative practices during computer writing in a first grade classroom.* Paper presented at the annual meeting of the American Educational Research Association, San Francisco.

Heller, N. (1991, December 10). Telecommunications makes a call. In The Technology Revolution Comes to Education, *Business Week*, pp. 94-96.

Herman, J. (1992). *Finding the reality behind the promise: Assessing the effects of technology in school reform.* Paper presented at SRI International's Conference on Technology and Education Reform, Dallas.

Herman, J., & Yeh, J. (1983). Some effects of parent involvement in schools. *The Urban Review, 15,* 11-17.

Holmes Group. (1990). *Tomorrow's schools: Principles for the design of professional development schools.* East Lansing, MI: Author.

Hopkins, M. (1991). Technologies as tools for transforming learning environments. *The Computing Teacher, 18*(7), 27-30.

Hoyles, C., & Noff, R. (1992). *Learning mathematics and LOGO.* Cambridge, MA: MIT Press.

Hunter, B. (1992). Linking for learning: Computer-and-communications network support for nationwide innovation in education. *Science Education and Technology, 1*(1), 23-34.

Johnston, J. (1987). *Electronic learning: From audiotape to videodisc.* Hillsdale, NJ: Erlbaum.

Johnston, J., & Ettma, J. (1986). Using television to best advantage: Research for prosocial television. In J. B. Bryant and D. Zillmann (Eds.), *Perspectives on media effects.* Hillsdale, NJ: Erlbaum.

Julyan, C. (1991). Getting connected to science. *Hands On!, 14*(1), 4-7.

Kitchen, W. (1987, March 11). *Education and telecommunications: Partners in progress* (ERIC, ED 282 551; testimony before the Senate Committee on Labor and Human Services).

Knapp, M. S., Adelman, N. E., Marder, C., McCollum, H., Needels, M. C., Shields, P. M., Turnbull, B. J., & Zucker, A. A. (1992). *Academic challenge for the children of poverty. Vol. 1: Findings and conclusions* (Contract LC88054001). Washington, DC: U.S. Department of Education, Office of Policy and Planning.

Knapp, M. S., Means, B., & Chelemer, C. (1991). Conclusion: Implementing new models for teaching advanced skills. In B. Means, C. Chelemer, & M. S. Knapp (Eds.), *Teaching advanced skills to at-risk students: Views from research and practice.* San Francisco: Jossey-Bass.

Knapp, M. S., & Turnbull, B. J. (1990). *Better schooling for the children of poverty: Alternatives to conventional wisdom. Vol. I: Summary.* Menlo Park, CA: SRI International.

Krendl, K. A., & Fredin, E. S. (1985). The effects of instructional design characteristics: An examination of two communication systems. *Journal of Educational Technology Systems, 14*(1), 75-86.

Kulik, J. A., Bangert, R. L., & Williams, G. W. (1983). Effects of computer-based teaching on secondary school students. *Journal of Educational Psychology, 75*, 19-26.

Kulik, C., Kulik, J., & Bangert-Drowns, R. L. (1984). *Effects of computer based education on secondary school pupils.* Paper presented at the annual meeting of the American Educational Research Association, New Orleans.

Kulik, J., Kulik, C.-L. C., & Bangert-Drowns, R. L. (1985). Effectiveness of computer-based education in elementary schools. *Computers in Human Behavior, 1*, 59-74.

Kurland, D. M. (1991). *TextBrowser: A computer-based instructional management and assessment system for language arts instruction*. Unpublished paper, Education Development Center, Newton, MA.

Lehrer, R. (1992). Authors of knowledge: Patterns of hypermedia design. In S. Lajoie & S. Derry (Eds.), *Computers as cognitive tools*. Hillsdale, NJ: Erlbaum.

Lehrer, R., Erickson, J., & Connell, T. (1992). *Assessing knowledge design*. Paper presented at the annual meeting of the American Educational Research Association, San Francisco.

Lenk, C. (1988). Doing science through telecommunications. In J. Ellis (Ed.), *Information technology and science education (AETS yearbook)*. Columbus, OH: Ohio State University, SMEAC Information Reference Center.

Lesgold, A., et al. (1992, January). *Report of a workshop on Educational Potential of Wideband National Network held at George Mason University, November 1-2, 1991*. (Supported by National Science Foundation Grant #MDR-9050259.) Pittsburgh, PA: University of Pittsburgh.

Levin, H. M. (1989). The economics of computer-assisted instruction. *Peabody Journal of Education, 64*(1), 52-66.

Levin, J., Boruta, M., & Vasconcellos, M. (1983). Microcomputer-based environments for writing: A writer's assistant. In A. C. Wilkinson (Ed.), *Classroom computers and cognitive science*. New York: Academic Press.

Levin, J. A., Kim, H., & Riel, M. M. (1990). Analyzing instructional interactions on electronic message networks. In L. M. Harasim (Ed.), *Online education: perspectives on a new environment* (pp. 185-213). New York: Praeger.

Levin, H. M., & Meister, G. R. (1985, November). *Educational technology and computers: Promises, promises, always promises* (Project Report No. 85-A13). Stanford, CA: Stanford University, Institute for Research on Educational Finance and Governance.

Levin, J. A., Waugh, M., Kim, H., & Miyake, N. (1990, April). *Learning in electronic networks: Global and local activity cycles*. Paper presented at the annual meeting of the American Educational Research Association, Boston.

Macrorie, K. (1988). *The I-Search paper*. Portsmouth, NH: Boynton/Cook.

Mageau, T. (1990). ILS: Its new role in schools. *Electronic Learning, 10*(1), 22-32.

Mageau, T. (1991a, Spring). Computer using teachers. *Agenda, 1*, 51.

Mageau, T. (1991b, Spring). Ten smart lessons for the '90s. *Agenda, 1*, 48-51.

Mokros, J. R., & Tinker, R. F. (1987). The impact of microcomputer-based labs on children's ability to interpret graphs. *Journal of Research in Science Teaching, 24* (4), 369-383.

Martin, L. (1987). Teachers' adoption of multimedia technologies for science and mathematics instruction. In R. D. Pea & K. Sheingold (Eds.), *Mirrors of minds: Patterns of experience in educational computing*. Norwood, NJ: Ablex.

Means, B., Chelemer, C., & Knapp, M. S. (1991). *Teaching advanced skills to at-risk students: Views from research and practice*. San Francisco: Jossey-Bass.

Means, B., Knapp, M. S., & Chelemer, C. (1991). Introduction: Rethinking teaching for disadvantaged students. In B. Means, C. Chelemer, & M. S. Knapp (Eds.), *Teaching advanced skills to at-risk students: Views from research and practice*. San Francisco: Jossey-Bass.

Mehan, D. (1989). Oracular reasoning in a psychiatric exam: The resolution of conflict in language. In A. D. Grimshaw (Ed.), *Conflict talk: Sociolinguistic investigations of arguments in conversation*. Cambridge: Cambridge University Press.

Moore, M. G. (1989, May). *Effects of distance learning: A summary of the literature* (NTIS Accession No. PB90-125238/XAB; prepared for the Office of Technology Assessment, Washington, DC). University Park, PA: Pennsylvania State University.

Morocco, C. C. (1991, April). *Integrating technology into interdisciplinary curricula in the middle school: What do teachers need to know?* Paper presented at the annual meeting of the American Educational Research Association, Chicago.

Morocco, C. C., & Dalton, B. (1990). *Learning disabled students in the regular science classroom: Case studies from the "Voyage of the Mimi."* Unpublished paper presented at Technology and Media Conference, Lexington, KY.

Morocco, C., Dalton, B., & Tivnan, T. (1989). *The impact of computer-supported writing instruction on the writing quality of learning disabled students* (Final report, EDC Writing Project). Newton, MA: Education Development Center.

Morocco, C., Dalton, B., & Tivnan, T. (1992). The impact of computer-supported writing environments on fourth-grade students with and without learning disabilities. *Reading and Writing Quarterly: Overcoming Learning Difficulties, 8*(1), 87-114.

Morrison, D., & Walters, J. (1989, June). *Immigrant: Who's using it*. Paper presented at the National Educational Computing Conference, Boston.

National Commission on Excellence in Education. (1983). *A nation at risk: The imperative for educational reform*. Washington, DC: Decision Resources Corporation.

Nelson, C. S., Watson, J. A., & Busch, J. C. (1989, Summer). The interactive videodisc as an educational tool. *Journal of Interactive Instruction Development*, pp. 11-16.

Nelson, R. N. (1985). Two-way microwave transmission consolidates, improves education. *NASSP Bulletin, 69*(484), 38-42.

Newman, D. (1990a). Opportunities for research on the organizational impact of school computers. *Educational Researcher, 19*(3), 8-13.

Newman, D. (1990b). Telecommunications: Using phone lines in the classroom. In C. Warger (Ed.), *Technology in today's schools*. Alexandria, VA: Association for Supervision and Curriculum Development.

Newman, D. (1992a, December). Technology as support for school structure and school restructuring. *Phi Delta Kappan*, pp. 308-315.

Newman, D. (1992b). *Turning telecomputing inside out*. Paper presented at the Conference on Technology and Education Reform, presented by SRI International, Dallas, TX.

Niemiec, R. P., & Walberg, H. J. (1985). Computers and achievement in the elementary schools. *Journal of Educational Computing Research, 1*(4), 435-440.

Oakes, J., & Schneider, M. (1984, November). Computers and schools: Another case of "...The more they stay the same"? *Educational Leadership*, pp. 73-79.

O'Connor, B. (1991, October). *Planning for the technology rich learning environments of the future* (Draft; prepared for the Council of Chief State School Officers Technology Leadership Conference, Dallas, TX). Sacramento, CA: California State University, Institute for the Study of Politics and Media.

Office of Technology Assessment, U.S. Congress. (1988). *Power on! New tools for teaching and learning*. Washington, DC: U.S. Government Printing Office.

Office of Technology Assessment, U.S. Congress. (1989, November). *Linking for learning: A new course for education*. Washington, DC: U.S. Government Printing Office.

Papert, S. (1980). *Mindstorms: Children, computers, and powerful ideas*. New York: Basic Books.

Pea, R. D. (1991, July). Learning through multimedia. *IEEE Computer Graphics and Applications*, pp. 58-66.

Pea, R. D., & Kurland, D. M. (1987). On the cognitive effects of learning computer programming. In R. D. Pea & K. Sheingold (Eds.), *Mirrors of minds: Patterns of experience in educational computing*, pp. 147-177.

Pellegrino, J. W., Hickey, D., Heath, A., Rewey, K., & Vye, N. J. (1992). *Assessing the outcomes of an innovative instructional program: The 1990-1991 implementation of the "Adventures of Jasper Woodbury."* Nashville, TN: Learning Technology Center, Vanderbilt University.

Piele, P. K. (1989). The politics of technology utilization. In D. E. Mitchell & M. E. Goertz (Eds.), *Education politics for the new century: The twentieth anniversary yearbook of the Politics of Education Association* (pp. 93-106). London: Falmer Press.

Pogrow, S. (1990, January). Challenging at-risk students: Findings from the HOTS program. *Phi Delta Kappan*, pp. 389-397.

Ray, D. (1991). Telephone conversation.

Resnick, L. B. (1987). *Education and learning to think.* Washington, DC: National Academy Press.

Riel, M. (1983). Education and ecstasy: Computer chronicles of students writing together. *The Quarterly Newsletter of the Laboratory of Comparative Human Cognition, 3,* 59-67.

Riel, M. (1989). The impact of computers in classrooms. *Journal of Research on Computing in Education, 22*(2), 180-189.

Riel, M. (1990a). Building a new foundation for global communities. *The Writing Notebook, 7,* 35-37.

Riel, M. (1990b). Cooperative learning across classrooms in electronic learning circles. *Instructional Science, 19,* 445-466.

Riel, M. (1990c, April). *Learning circles: A model for educational telecomputing.* Paper presented at the annual meeting of the American Educational Research Association, Boston.

Riel, M. (1991a). Computer mediated communication: A tool for reconnecting kids with society. *Interactive Learning Environments, 1*(4), 255-263.

Riel, M. (1991b). Learning circles around the globe. *The Writing Notebook, 8*(3), 38.

Riel, M. (1992, January). *AT&T Learning Circle.* Presentation at Symposium in Technology & Social Interaction, International Conference, Technology and Media (TAM), Division of the Council for Exceptional Children, Albuquerque.

Riel, M., & Levin, J. A. (1990). Building electronic communities: Success and failure in computer networking. *Instructional Science, 19*(2), 145-169.

Rockman, S. (1991, October-November). *To lead or to follow: The role and influence of research on technology*. Paper commissioned for the Chief State School Officers' State Technology Leadership Conference, Dallas.

Rosegrant, T. (1986). Using the computer as a scaffold for assisting beginning readers and writers. In J. Hoot (Ed.), *Computers in early childhood education: Issues and practices*. Englewood Cliffs, NJ: Prentice Hall.

Rosenholtz, S. J. (1985, May). Effective schools: Interpreting the evidence. *American Journal of Education, 93*(3), 352-389.

Rubin, A., & Bruce, B. (1985). Quill: Reading and writing with a microcomputer. In B. A. Hutson (Ed.), *Advances in reading/language research, Vol. III*. Greenwich, CT: JAI Press.

Salomon, G. (1984). Television is "easy" and print is "tough": The differential investment of mental effort in learning as a function of perceptions and attributions. *Journal of Educational Psychology, 76*(4), 647-658.

Salomon, G. (1991). Transcending the qualitative-quantitative debate: The analytic and systemic approaches to educational research. *Educational Researcher, 20*(6), 10-18.

Samson, G. E., Niemiec, R., Weinstein, T., & Walberg, H. J. (1986, Summer). Effects of computer-based instruction on secondary school achievement: A quantitative synthesis. *AEDS Journal*, pp. 312-326.

Scardamalia, M., Bereiter, C., McLean, R. S., Swallow, J., & Woodruff, E. (1989). Computer-supported intentional learning environments. *Journal of Educational Computing Research, 5*(1), 51-68.

Schofield, J. W., Evans-Rhodes, D., & Huber, B. R. (1989). *Artificial intelligence in the classroom: The impact of a computer-based tutor on teachers and students* (Contract No. N00014-85-K-0664). Arlington, VA: Office of Naval Research, Cognitive Science Program.

Schulz, E. (1992, January 8). Learning a hard lesson on the introduction of technology. *Education Week*, pp. 18-20.

Sheekey, A. D., & Douglas, S. G. (1991). Telecommunications: The critical resource for achieving national educational goals. In A. D. Sheekey (Ed.), *Education policy and telecommunications technologies*. Washington, DC: Office of Educational Research and Improvement.

Shields, P. M. (1990). A review of research on school and community influences on effective curriculum and instruction. In M. S. Knapp & P. M. Shields (Eds.), *Better schooling for the children of poverty: Alternatives to conventional wisdom. Vol. II: Commissioned papers and literature review* (pp. XIII-1 – XIII-15). Washington, DC: U.S. Department of Education, Office of Planning, Budget and Evaluation.

Sheingold, K. (1990, December). Restructuring for learning with technology: The potential for synergy. *Restructuring for Learning with Technology*, pp. 9-27.

Sheingold, K. (1991a). Restructuring for learning with technology: The potential for synergy. *Phi Delta Kappan, 73*(1), 17-27.

Sheingold, K. (1991b, October). *Toward an alternative teaching environment.* (Draft for Technology Leadership Conference, Council of Chief State School Officers, Dallas).

Sheingold, K., & Hadley, M. (1990). *Accomplished teachers: Integrating computers into classroom practice.* New York: Bank Street College of Education, Center for Technology in Education.

Sheingold, K., & Tucker, M. S. (Eds.). (1990, December). *Restructuring for learning with technology.* New York: Bank Street College of Education, Center for Technology in Education; and Rochester, NY: National Center on Education and the Economy.

Sherwood, R. D., Kinzer, C. K., Bransford, J. D., & Franks, J. J. (1987). Some benefits of creating macro-contexts for science instruction: Initial findings. *Journal of Research in Science Teaching, 24*(5), 415-435.

Shulman, L. S. (1986). Paradigms and research programs in the study of teaching: A contemporary perspective. In M. C. Wittrock (Ed.), *Handbook of research on teaching* (pp. 3-36). New York: Macmillan.

Slavin, R. E. (1991). Reading effects of IBM's "Writing to Read" program: A review of evaluations. *Educational Evaluation and Policy Analysis, 13*(1), 1-11.

Sleeman, D. (1985). Basic algebra revisited: A study with 14 year olds. *International Journal of Man-Machine Studies, 22*(2), 127-149.

Sleeman, D., & Brown, J. S. (Eds.). (1982). *Intelligent tutoring systems.* London: Academic Press.

Smith, L. S., Chlebicki, A. N., & Hartman, P. A. (1991, June). *Using hypermedia to implement curricular change.* Paper presented at the National Educational Computing Conference, Phoenix.

Smith, M. S., & O'Day, J. (1990). Systemic school reform. In *Politics of Education Association yearbook* (pp. 233-267). London: Taylor & Francis.

Soloway, E. (1991). How the Nintendo generation learns. *Communications of the ACM, 34*(9), 23-26, 95.

Spoehr, K. T. (1992). *Using hypermedia to clarify conceptual structures: Illustrations from history and literature.* Paper presented at the annual meeting of the American Educational Research Association, San Francisco.

Stearns, M. S., David, J. L., Hanson, S. G., Ringstaff, C., & Schneider, S. A. (1991, January). *Cupertino-Fremont Model Technology Schools Project research findings: Executive summary (Teacher-centered model of technology integration: End of year 3).* Menlo Park, CA: SRI International.

Stearns, P. H. (1991a, June). *Explore, discover, present! Technology in the social studies classroom.* Paper presented at the National Educational Computing Conference, Phoenix.

Stearns, P. H. (1991b). Point of view. *The Computing Teacher, 18*(6), 41-46.

Stearns, P. H. (1991c). Telephone conversation.

Stearns, P. H. (In press). Preparing learning disabled students for success in the information age. *The Computing Teacher.*

Suppes, P. (1980). The teacher and computer-assisted instruction. In R. Taylor (Ed.) *The computer in the school: Tutor, tool, tutee* (pp. 231-235). New York: Teachers College Press.

Sutton, R. E. (1991). Equity and computers in the schools: A decade of research. *Review of Educational Research, 61*(4), 475-503.

Technical Education Research Centers (TERC). (1990). *The National Geographic Kids Network, year 4 final annual report.* Cambridge, MA: Author.

Technology-aided teaching spreads to schools nationwide. (1991, March 22). *Education Daily,* p. 2.

Tinker, R., & Papert, S. (1989). Tools for science education. In J. D. Ellis (Ed.), *1988 AETS yearbook, information technology and science education.* Columbus, OH: Association for the Education of Teachers in Science and ERIC Clearinghouse for Science, Mathematics and Environmental Education.

Walters, J., & Gardner, H. (1990). *Computer domain projects: A new approach to achieving expertise in diverse spheres of knowledge (Second annual report to the John and Mary R. Markle Foundation).* Cambridge, MA: Project Zero.

Walters, J., & Gardner, H. (1991). *Final report to the Markle Foundation*. Cambridge, MA: Project Zero.

West, P. (1991, June 19). Bill aims to tap educational benefits of fiber-optic telecommunications. *Education Week*, p. 28.

Whitehead, A. N. (1929). *The aims of education*. New York: Macmillan.

Wilson, K. S. (1987). *The Palenque optical disc prototype: Design of multimedia experiences for education and entertainment in a nontraditional learning context* (Technical Report No. 44). New York: Bank Street College of Education, Center for Children and Technology.

Wilson, K. S., & Tally, W. J. (1991). *Designing for discovery: Interactive multimedia learning environments at Bank Street College* (Technical Report No. 15). New York: Bank Street College of Education, Center for Technology in Education.

Wiske, M. S. (1990, April). *Teaching geometry through guided inquiry: A case of changing mathematics instruction with new technologies*. Paper presented at the annual meeting of the American Educational Research Association, Boston.

Wiske, M. S., & Houde, R. (1988). *From recitation to construction: Teachers change with new technologies* (Technical Report TR88-28). Cambridge, MA: Harvard Graduate School of Education, Educational Technology Center.

Wiske, M. S., Niguidula, D., & Shepard, J. W. (1988). *Collaborative research goes to school: Guided inquiry with computers in classrooms* (Technical Report TR 88-1). Cambridge, MA: Harvard Graduate School of Education, Educational Technology Center.

Wiske, M. S., Zodhiates, P., Wilson, B., Gordon, M., Harvey, W., Krensky, L., Lord, B., Watt, M., & Williams, K. (1988, March). *How technology affects teaching* (Technical report prepared for the Office of Technology Assessment, Congress of the United States). Cambridge, MA: Harvard Graduate School of Education, Educational Technology Center.

Yerushalmy, M., Chazan, D., & Gordon, M. (1988). *Guided inquiry and technology: A yearlong study of children and teachers using the Geometric Supposer* (Technical Report No. 90-8). Newton, MA: Education Development Center.

Yerushalmy, M., Chazan, D., & Gordon, M. (1990). *Guided inquiry and technology: A yearlong study of children and teachers using the Geometric Supposer* Newton, MA: Education Development Center, Center for Learning Technology.

Yoder, S. K. (1991, October 21). Readin', writin' and multimedia. *The Wall Street Journal*, p. R12.

Zellermayer, M., Salomon, G., Globerson, T., & Givon, H. (1991). Enhancing writing-related metacognitions through a computerized writing partner. *American Educational Research Journal, 28*(2), 373-391.

Zorfass, J. M. (1991, April). *Promoting successful technology integration through active teaching practices.* Paper presented at the annual meeting of the American Educational Research Association, Chicago.

Zorfass, J. M., Morocco, C. C., & Lory, N. (1991). *A school-based approach to technology integration.* In *ASCD curriculum handbook.* Alexandria, VA: Association for Supervision and Curriculum Development, Curriculum/Technology Resource Center.

Zorfass, J., Morocco, C. C., Russell, S. J., & Zuman, J. (1989). *Evaluation of the integration of technology for instructing handicapped children (middle school level) (Phase I final report).* Newton, MA: Education Development Center.

Zorfass, J., Morocco, C. C., Tivnan, T., Persky, S., & Remz, A. R. (1991). *Evaluation of the integration of technology for instructing handicapped children (middle school level) (Phase II final report).* Newton, MA: Education Development Center.